HOW TO OPEN
and successfully operate
A COUNTRY INN

OTHER INN AND TRAVEL BOOKS
FROM BERKSHIRE HOUSE PUBLISHERS

The Innkeepers Collection Cookbook by C. Vincent Shortt

The Red Lion Inn Cookbook by Suzi Forbes Chase

Country Inns and Back Roads Cookbook by Norman Simpson and
the staff of Berkshire Traveller Press

The GREAT DESTINATIONS™ Series

The Berkshire Book: A Complete Guide

The Santa Fe & Taos Book: A Complete Guide

The Napa & Sonoma Book: A Complete Guide

The Chesapeake Bay Book: A Complete Guide

The Coast of Maine Book: A Complete Guide

The Adirondack Book: A Complete Guide

The Aspen Book: A Complete Guide

The Charleston, Savannah & Coastal Islands Book: A Complete Guide

The Gulf Coast of Florida Book: A Complete Guide

The Central Coast of California: A Complete Guide

The Newport & Narragansett Bay Book: A Complete Guide

The Hamptons Book: A Complete Guide

HOW TO OPEN
and successfully operate
A COUNTRY INN

BY C. VINCENT SHORTT

Based on the classic original of the same title
by Karen L. Etsell and Elaine C. Brennan

Berkshire House Publishers
Stockbridge, Massachusetts

HOW TO OWN AND SUCCESSFULLY OPERATE A COUNTRY INN
by C. Vincent Shortt

Copyright © 1993 by Berkshire House Publishers
Original edition © 1981, l983 by Karen L. Etsell and Elaine C. Brennan

Library of Congress Cataloging-in-Publishing Data
Shortt, C. Vincent
    How to open and successfuly operate a country Inn / C. Vincent Shortt.
        p.   cm.
    Rev. ed. of: How to open a country inn / Karen L. Etsell & Elaine C. Brennan. c. 1981.
    Includes bibliographical references and index.
    ISBN 0-936399-41-4 : $14.95
    1. Hotel management. I. Etsell, Karen L. How to open a country inn. II. Title.
TX911.3.M27S47   1993
647.94'068–dc20   93-25666
                                                            CIP

Photographs appear by courtesy of the individual inns and credited photographers.
Editor: Deborah Burns
Cover and book design: Jane McWhorter

Berkshire House books are available at substantial discounts for bulk purchases by corporations and other organizations for promotions and premiums. Special personalized editions can also be produced in large quantities.
For more information, contact:

Berkshire House Publishers
Box 297, Stockbridge MA 01262
800-321-8526

Manufactured in the United States of America
10 9 8 7 6 5 4 3 2

This book is dedicated to a person I never met. In every field of endeavor there are single-minded dreamers who, by sheer force of will and love for people, succeed in creating timeless monuments.

Norman T. Simpson found his vocation when his love for the road less traveled, and his boundless enthusiasm for discovering what made every innkeeper special, merged in *Country Inns and Back Roads* to kindle today's broad public enthusiasm for country inns and the people who own and operate them.

Happy trails, Norman.

CONTENTS

Introduction

"This isn't a business," an innkeeper once told me, "it's a love affair." For Ann and me, our love affair with inns began in the spring of 1972, when we visited the Maritime Provinces of Canada.

Just west of the border between Nova Scotia and New Brunswick is a college town called Sackville, New Brunswick. We decided to try a splendid little country place called Marshlands Inn. We have never forgotten the warmth of the staff . . . the cookies and hot chocolate on the front porch . . . the smell of their fresh-baked bread . . . our first taste of fiddlehead greens . . . or Marshlands' signature rack of lamb served with finely chopped peanuts and freshly grated coconut.

We were hooked. The opportunity to share the hospitality of a place with warm and thoughtful people soon became our favorite lodging choice wherever we travel. Since that trip we have enjoyed country inns throughout North America and Europe, and we've marveled at the enormous increase in the number and quality of superb properties — particularly in the past ten years.

In 1992, my love affair with inns and innkeepers became a public matter when I created the first television series in history devoted to America's great country inns. With the development of our series, "Inn Country USA," and the opportunity to meet several hundred of the finest innkeepers in the business over the past few years, came the idea for this book.

When the decision was made to update *How to Open and Successfully Operate a Country Inn*, it was decided to anchor the new book in the real world of innkeepers. Any "How-to" book author would feel woefully unprepared to address an industry as complex as this one without the support, guidance, and contributions of not one but several of the most successful people currently in the business. The Innkeepers' Roundtable featured in this book is a sampling of professional innkeepers across America. Located from Eureka, California, to Savannah, Georgia, these entrepreneurs share the basic problems of any small business person in the nation today. The challenges of capitalization, personnel, and marketing that face the country innkeeper on a day-to-day basis are not very different from those facing the neighborhood restaurant, florist, or printer.

What makes innkeeping unique is the role played by the stars of this play — the innkeepers. Although they come in all shapes, sizes, and ages, and occupy a variety of old and new inns, innkeepers have in common some "golden threads." They love people, and they take great pleasure and pride in serving others.

As you will discover, however, successful innkeepers are busy people, so not many of them have time even to consider putting their years of experience into words of wisdom for the aspiring innkeeper. All the members of our Innkeepers' Roundtable were kind enough to "live" for a few weeks with a voice-activated microcassette recorder into which they dictated their contributions to this book. If you feel as if you're sitting next to them as they speak, that's because in a sense you are. Their comments, wherever possible, have been transcribed precisely as they made them. Their candor, humor, and warmth remain intact for you to enjoy between now and your next visit to their country inn. HAPPY TRAILS!

THE INNKEEPERS' ROUNDTABLE

With great pleasure, we introduce the members of our Innkeeper's Roundtable:

The Carter House, Eureka, California. Mark and Christie Carter are the only members of the Innkeepers' Roundtable who actually constructed their own inn. They originally built the Carter House as their private residence, meticulously designed and constructed as a copy of an 1884 San Francisco Victorian mansion. Their inn business has grown over the past ten years to occupy three separate structures with thirty guest rooms.

The Gastonian, Savannah, Georgia. In 1985, Hugh and Roberta Lineberger spent their life savings (and their retirement nest egg) to acquire, elegantly restore, and completely refurnish two adjoining 1868 Victorian homes in historic old Savannah. The Gastonian, with thirteen rooms and suites, is now the only inn in Georgia, and one of the few in the Southeast, that has earned both the Mobil 4 Star and the AAA 4 Diamond awards for operating excellence. Hugh and Roberta never looked back.

The Grant Corner Inn, Santa Fe, New Mexico. In 1981 Pat Walter, his wife Louise Stewart, and their five-year-old daughter "Bumpy" restored a charming 1905 Victorian house just a block away from the old square in old Santa Fe. Their popular thirteen-room country inn is a true family success story.

The Governor's Inn, Ludlow, Vermont. By any standard, Deedy and Charlie Marble have elevated their eight-room, turn-of-the-century Victorian inn in this village of 2,500 people to the Inngoers' Hall of Fame. Their operating creativity and marketing savvy are evident everywhere you turn, from *Yankee* magazine to the back of the Country Inn Rice box in your kitchen cabinet.

The Vermont Inn, Killington, Vermont. Judd and Susan Levy left the fast lane of New York investment banking on August 1, 1988, to become the proud owners and operators of a nineteen-room country inn with a successful fifty-seat restaurant. The Vermont Inn was an operating inn in need of the talent, taste, energy, and enthusiasm the Levys brought to this four-season resort community.

The Oaks, Christiansburg, Virginia. Tom and Margaret Ray have literally brought innkeeping to this beautiful southwestern Virginia community. Their century-old frame classic Victorian with giant oak trees dominating the lawn has become the centerpiece of Christiansburg lodging and gracious entertaining in the few years since the Rays moved to town.

The Inn at Sawmill Farm, West Dover, Vermont. Rod, Ione, and Brill Williams own and operate the only Relais & Chateau country inn represented in our roundtable. As innkeeping veterans (they began converting the old dairy farm to a twenty-room inn during their Christmas vacation in 1966), and pioneers in the fraternity of fine Vermont innkeepers, the Williamses' perspective on the industry is as rich and original as their famous spicy homemade tomato juice.

The White Oak Inn, 60 miles northeast of Columbus, Ohio. Joyce and Jim Acton decided in 1985 to pursue their dream of becoming Ohio innkeepers. After a professional life of constant senior management travel and stress for both, they were eager to get underway with their ten-room inn. The Actons are now former innkeepers — the only ones on our roundtable — and their first-hand insight into the profession made a valuable addition to this book.

Part One

GETTING STARTED

RICHARD SMALTZ

Tara, a country inn in the tradition of Gone with the Wind, *in Clark, Pennsylvania.*

Chapter One

KNOW YOUR INDUSTRY

THE CHANGING HOSPITALITY INDUSTRY

Ever since humans first created and moved into their own shelters from the weather, they have been sharing their homes with their extended families and their friends. As early as A.D. 961, a group of Swiss Augustinian monks took the idea even further when they established a seventy-five-bed inn in a narrow Alpine pass on the road to Rome.

The hospitality industry has grown to become the largest employer in the world, with restaurants and lodging facilities dominating our contemporary landscape. The proliferation of establishments catering to the traveling public has led to a variety of specialized food, beverage, and lodging concepts. Dramatically increased costs of real estate, construction, and marketing have resulted in multi-unit lodging chains scrambling to broaden their reach and their appeal.

When Kemmons Wilson became frustrated by the lack of consistency in the roadside lodging establishments he and his family visited during a cross-country family vacation in the 1950s, he returned home to Memphis and opened the first Holiday Inn. With its ubiquitous green, white, and yellow roadside sign, the Holiday Inn has evolved into a multi-layered family of lodging concepts.

Vertically integrated (that's marketing talk for how many different ways one company can creatively appeal to people at all levels of income and taste) lodging companies abound. Ramada Inns, for example, have gone upscale (and higher priced) with their Renaissance concepts. Choice Hotels also has something for everyone — Comfort Inns, Quality Inns, Clarion Hotels, Sleep Inns, Rodeway Inns, Econo Lodge, and Friendship Inns, with a total of 217,209 guest rooms. Many hotels have even fragmented their product within their own four walls by offering "top shelf" service and added amenities to guests who are willing to pay the added premium.

But while the major chains scramble to be all things to all people in all price ranges, one segment of the hospitality industry remains low-key and discreet — innkeeping. And it is the largest and arguably the fastest-growing segment provider of overnight lodging in the hospitality industry.

Like every other segment of the hospitality industry, however, the business of innkeeping has changed a great deal over the past twenty years. In 1965, a warm and gregarious former advertising executive named Norman Simpson wrote a sixteen-page book describing twelve inns in informal, richly descriptive prose and called it *Country Inns and Back Roads*. The publishing success story of *Country Inns and Back Roads*, now an annual publication covering hundreds of inns, reflects the true renaissance of the American village inn.

The year after *Country Inns and Back Roads* was first published, one of our roundtable members, the Inn at Sawmill Farm, began its transformation into one of America's most highly regarded country inns. As owner/innkeeper Rod Williams explains, getting into the business of innkeeping in 1966 was quite a different proposition than it is today.

"Like a lot of early innkeepers, our passion for this business grew out of our passion for visiting other inns. As an avid skiing family, we had visited inns and ski lodges all over the world, so we felt we had a good idea of what the business was all about. Of course, as it turned out we had a lot to learn. But since we were one of the first innkeeping families in Vermont, we had very little competition in the early days, so we had the luxury of learning the business as we went along."

Higher up-front investments for buildings and land, more sophisticated marketing techniques, better trained and equipped innkeepers, and a dramatic increase in the number of inns of all sizes and descriptions all over America have combined with an increasingly discriminating and demanding inngoing public to make the "learn as you go" method of owning and operating a successful country inn a rarity today.

By 1980 there were an estimated 2,000 B&Bs and country inns in America. Today, the figure has risen to 20,000, and the inn segment of the hospitality industry turns down the covers for more than 20,000,000 visitors each year. From all indications, the business of innkeeping is indeed on a roll.

The Future of the Inn Business

The future success of the country inn industry rests in its continuing movement from an avocational to a vocational business. As more and more bed and breakfast inns evolve into full-service country inns, and these full-service facilities continue to broaden their hospitality to keep up with the expectations of the inn-going public, the quality of the overall inn experience will improve. This is not to say there are not some superb, highly professional B&Bs out there serving the public well, but, ultimately, the full-service country inn segment of the industry will be the driving force behind the continued growth of the business.

As the high-profile leader of the industry, country inns themselves have begun to evolve into their own areas of specialization. Gourmet cooking classes, nearby nature trails, historic antiquity, and antique tableware have all been used as points of differentiation by enterprising innkeepers seeking their own competitive advantage. Country inns that specialize in serving precisely defined demographic subsets of the traveling public, such as single women or cross-country bicycle groups, have begun to emerge in an increasingly crowded competitive arena.

COMING TO TERMS

Like a lot of industries, innkeeping has its own language and vocabulary. We have tried to use terms that are generally understood and acceptable to the industry, but in some cases our definitions may differ slightly from yours. Since our objective is to assist you in successfully opening and operating a country inn, let's begin there.

Country Inns

A country inn is a lodging facility with from five to nineteen overnight guest rooms. The country inn traditionally serves at least one meal in addition to breakfast and has a food service component that is often open to the general public as well as to inn guests. The full-service restaurant is frequently licensed to sell alcoholic beverages. The country innkeeper generally operates the inn as a full-time or nearly full-time pursuit, and often lives on or adjacent to the property.

The definition that best captures the essence of a country inn, however, is not the one that describes the facility, its meal service, or its operating hours. If you've experienced many country inns, you know that an inn experience is more than an overnight stay in a lovely old home with a sumptuous breakfast and an unforgettable rack of lamb dinner. Each country inn is a distinctive, highly personalized statement of the identity, style, and taste of the innkeeper. Everything from interior decor, accessories, and food to the selection of magazines and books is an expression of the innkeeper's personality.

One roundtable member recalled the early advice of another experienced innkeeper: "Be yourself. Create an environment that pleases you first and then your inn will successfully and honestly mirror your personal taste. You cannot pretend to be something you are not twenty-four hours a day, seven days a week — don't even try!"

B&Bs, Homestays, and Small Hotels

In addition to country inns, several other segments of the industry serve an increasingly discerning traveling public with less emphasis on the full-service restaurant aspect of the business. Bed and breakfast inns and homestays are also typically owner-operated and often owner-occupied businesses, generally smaller in size than country inns. The bed and breakfast inn is usually a licensed business offering breakfast service with each night's lodging. Homestays are the least structured operations in this category. They generally offer lodging in one or two spare bedrooms, merchandise their accommodations through third-party reservation services, and do not have prominent exterior signage.

On the opposite end of the spectrum from the informal, often unregulated homestay businesses are small hotels. Small hotels are generally not owner-occupied and may or may not offer food as part of the lodging arrangement. They have twenty or more guest rooms and typically offer a full array of food and beverage services as well as a range of recreation venues, such as tennis courts, swimming pools, and jogging trails.

COUNTRY INN NETWORKING

Professional Associations

One indication of the maturity of this industry is the fact that support groups and associations have emerged to serve the innkeeper at all levels. As you explore the possibility of becoming a country innkeeper, it would be a good idea to make contact with the associations listed in Appendix A on pages 213–221.

If you cannot locate an association near you, try one or more of the national associations listed and request their criteria for membership, along with any materials they might have for aspiring innkeepers. No such list can be absolutely current because new associations are being established every day, so ask around for information on associations near you.

Innkeepers have learned that they are more likely to be heard on such issues as liability insurance, legislative concerns, and regional marketing matters when they are able to unite and speak with a common voice about the issues that affect them most. Your research into the country inn industry should certainly include active participation in one or more national, regional, and/or local innkeeper associations. Our roundtable reached unanimous consent on the importance of these professional support groups:

"We have found the professional organizations that support our industry to be a vital part of our success in the business. As founding members of the New Mexico B&B Association, we have helped articulate the standards for B&B operations in our area."

Once you're in business, *The B&B Industry Sourcebook*, published by the American Bed and Breakfast Association, has an entire section on establishing your own local association. You'll find help every step of the way in creating your own association, from establishing bylaws to handling association revenues.

Newsletters

Depending on your timetable for opening your country inn, it would make sense for you to look at the leading newsletters that specialize in innkeeping at all levels of the industry. These newsletters are generally published on a monthly, bimonthly, or quarterly basis and contain a lot of up-to-the-minute information on the profession.

We've listed several of the more informative publications in Appendix B on page 222. Some are available on a straight subscription basis; others are provided at no charge to their own membership body. For complete information on the publications and the segment of the industry each serves, contact the publishers directly. Many of these dedicated professionals are personal friends of ours, so give them our best regards and tell them where you found their names!

Libraries and Book Stores

Investigate the business of keeping a country inn with the same energy you'd invest in researching a new hobby or changing careers — because you are about to do both. Your local library and the book sellers in your community offer a large array of material on this inviting lifestyle, some of it more helpful than others, but all written by people with a genuine desire to entertain and inform you.

Don't Be Afraid to Ask!

As you begin to make contact with the resources outlined in this book, and you increase your personal contact with innkeepers, you will discover that innkeepers take great pleasure in sharing. That includes even the commodity that they treasure most — their time. Every innkeeper you will meet has one life experience in common with you. They too were once "Innkeeper Wannabes." Later on we'll talk in some detail about separating the fantasy from reality, but for now let's discuss how, and how not, to approach your most important resource in the field of country innkeeping: the innkeeper.

It is difficult to imagine another profession where the principals would be more forthcoming and open about sharing their world with an interested outsider. But as in any other all-consuming profession, certain times of the day are inconvenient for speaking informally with innkeepers about their profession. The more sensitive you are about those particularly busy times of the day, the more cooperative you are likely to find your innkeeper. Although it's their nature to be courteous, you'll get a much more attentive response to your questions if you avoid the hectic times such as breakfast or dinner service, check-in, and check-out.

It's a good idea to start your research of a particular inn or innkeeper by visiting as a guest first. This visit will make you better prepared to ask questions that are relevant to that particular operation. In the event you are not planning to visit the inn as a guest, it would be a much appreciated gesture to write an introductory note first, and follow it up with a late morning or early afternoon telephone call to arrange a convenient time to speak with the innkeeper.

ADVICE FROM THE EXPERTS

"Innkeepers are like swans on a placid lake. On the surface all appears idyllic and smooth, while beneath the surface they're paddling furiously to get from one task to the next."

"The most accurate description of an inn is that you are a parent and you have this great sense of pride in what is in essence your child. You get to nourish this creation and watch it grow and prosper. It's really that close a relationship."

Here are a few tidbits of advice from our roundtable to get you started researching this industry. We've pulled no punches here — so if you're still with us after these candid words, we'll roll up our sleeves in Chapter Two and begin a more detailed discussion of your particular market.

"I'd say if someone just gave you a couple million dollars, there are probably at least a couple million better ways to spend it than opening an inn!"

"I admit it. We're absolutely addicted to the positive feelings we get when we've put a smile on a guest's face."

"Travel around and stay in inns . . . it's a lot cheaper than owning one."

"Even though we're reasonably successful, we find ourselves constantly reinvesting whatever money we make back into the business."

"We may not get rich at it, but as long as we continue to get as much fulfillment from serving other people as we do today . . . we'll be innkeepers."

Growing public awareness of country inns has significantly increased the number of guests who aspire to become innkeepers. Several roundtable members estimated that as many as seven out of ten guests express a desire to enter the inn business sometime during their stay. One measure of an innkeeper's success has to be the frequency with which the guest expresses this desire.

"We often have guests who have been thoroughly steeped in the Bob Newhart school of innkeeping — and based purely on the romantic folly of a weekly half-hour sitcom, they have decided that this is the lifestyle for them.
"The first thing I tell them is DON'T DO IT!! But if they persist I'll tell them that it is the greatest thing that ever happened to us. It has truly made us alive again."

"Probably half of our guests express some interest in getting into the inn business. Most of them express that to us when we are all dressed for dinner and enjoying each other's company in the parlor prior to being seated in the dining room."

What the guest does not see are the backed-up sewage lines, drippy faucets, leaky roofs, sick staff, piles of wood waiting to be chopped, and all the other details of running this business.

Since it is difficult to appreciate fully what goes on in the real world of innkeeping without wearing the innkeeper's shoes, it would be an excellent idea to work in an inn before you decide to invest in one. Join one of the professional groups . . . learn the business from the bottom up. This business is not as easy as it looks.

"I would certainly encourage a close friend to consider the business of innkeeping, but I would say you must spend time working in an inn before taking the plunge. This does not mean being a guest, but actually working. I'd also tell them they would have to have access to a considerable pool of funds. Innkeeping is an expensive proposition. And finally, I would urge anyone getting into this business to take good care of themselves emotionally and physically."

An All-Encompassing Job

No segment of the hospitality industry demands more entrepreneurial energy and self-motivation than innkeeping. The size of the typical country inn and the need to staff as conservatively as possible often force the country innkeeper to be head chef, gracious host or hostess, venture capitalist, plumber, and salesman — all at the same time.

One innkeeper described his job as being like that of a bus driver on a mountainous narrow route known only by him. When he fails to show up for work the route just doesn't get covered. As the master of all trades within your country inn you have a heavy responsibility. The realization that you are the only one who can run the inn can be sobering indeed. Those innkeepers who have left companies and corporate jobs behind to pursue their dreams often remark about the extraordinary demands of the profession.

"We've seen too many people decide to 'cash in their chips' and leave the fast lane to pursue their lifelong dream of buying the 'perfect little inn.' Unfortunately, when getting out of the rat race is the primary motivation for opening an inn, the end result is often personal and financial disaster."

"Unless you've actually operated an inn, you cannot understand what virtual immersion in this business all day every day means in terms of constant fatigue. You are frequently up late awaiting the arrival of a guest, and up early the next morning preparing the breakfast — day in and day out."

Like any other entrepreneur running a new business, an innkeeper frequently puts the needs of the inn above his or her own personal needs.

From a former high-powered jet-setting senior management person turned innkeeper, here is an insight into how all-consuming the innkeeping business can become: *"I would actually feel guilty if I took two or three hours out of a day to pursue a personal matter or a hobby."* If it did not pertain directly to the inn, then this young grandfather did not feel right spending time on it.

This dedication is perhaps the most dramatic double-edged sword in the inn business. On one hand, the personal attention to every detail is what makes the inn experience so attractive for so many people. Unfortunately, it also accounts for the burnout of literally hundreds of hard-working, well-intentioned innkeepers each year.

"If I had it to do over again — knowing what I know now — I wouldn't do it. The drain on our personal lives was enormous, and for us, the business was frankly a money pit. Even though we did OK financially when we sold the inn, in retrospect there are a lot of other ways we could have invested our money and our energies and made considerably more money with less effort and personal sacrifice."

When is it a good idea to ignore even good advice? When your heart speaks louder than your head. One of our roundtable members admitted that probably the most valuable advice he received before purchasing his country inn was the advice not to do it — *"but we ignored the advice and now five years later we are glad that we did. Fortunately for us we chose to follow quite closely the second best advice we received, and that has really paid off — be yourself!"*

Trying the Job On

Without exception the most commonly voiced career advice we heard in our research was: *"Do your homework — so you'll go into the business with more realistic expectations."* (Note: The book you have in your hands right now indicates you have taken this advice to heart!)

Get to know innkeeping from both sides of the door. The consensus among successful innkeepers is that too many people look at innkeeping only from the consumer or inn-guest perspective. While the guest's view is certainly a fine place to begin, and in fact is where most of us begin our love affair with this industry, it should not be the only perspective you bring to the table before investing several hundred thousand dollars and five or ten years of your life.

"Making the decision to enter the inn business based on the delightful ten or twelve first-hand inn experiences you've had over the past several years is like deciding to buy a pineapple plantation because you've fallen in love with pineapple upside-down cake. You owe it to yourself and your family to research the industry as much as you possibly can before you make the final decision to make it your life's work."

Unlike most other attractive professions, such as investment banking, brain surgery, or detective work, you can actually "try on" innkeeping to see if it fits before you take the plunge. Through careful research and a little elbow grease, you can get a genuine feel for what it's like to run a country inn.

Volunteer to work in an inn in your area. Do all the jobs required of an innkeeper and concentrate on doing them well. It is only through first-hand experience that you'll learn which tasks you most enjoy and which you prefer to hire others to do for you.

This idea of trying out innkeeping has even created a subset of innkeepers who call themselves "innsitters." These entrepreneurs have discovered they can travel to interesting places, and be innkeepers, by offering to take care of the inn while the innkeepers take their regular vacations. Clearly, the concept of innsitting is not for everyone — and it is not for the inexperienced.

When you visit inns, don't just concentrate on the physical characteristics of the property such as wallpaper, paint selection, or accessories. Observe the innkeepers carefully. Get a sense of how they handle their time and their guests. If possible, let the innkeeper know in advance that you are researching the possibility of getting into the business, and you would appreciate a few minutes of their time. Innkeepers are people who love people — and that includes those who have been hopelessly bitten by the innkeeping "bug." Just make sure you have your conversation at their convenience and not yours!

Now that you've begun your research into the industry, don't stop. The bottom line to getting to know this industry is a personal one. You must have an intuitive love for people and a deep respect for the privilege of serving them. If you lack either, you will resent the financial and personal demands this industry will place on you. But if you've decided innkeeping sounds like your "cup of tea," come along and get to know the profession on a first-name basis.

The Successful Innkeeper

When someone persists in seeking advice on the business, the Number One bit of advice is that you had better like — no, love — people. That is paramount. "A love of antiques, decorating, collecting, food, and entertaining will serve you well as an innkeeper," said one roundtable member, "but a dedication to personal service is the single most important factor in determining whether you'll still be innkeeping ten years from now."

Next, the successful country innkeeper must be dedicated to excellence. Finally, the ongoing financial commitment to renewing the property was emphasized by another roundtable member: "Unless you are willing to make the personal sacrifices and financial investment necessary to constantly update your decor, and to operate a first-rate dining room, then you should consider something other than a country inn."

RIKKI THOMPSON

A luxurious bath pampers guests at the White Lake Inn, Sturgeon Bay, Wisconsin.

Chapter Two

KNOW YOUR MARKET

The Lodging Market
    Not All Markets Are Created Equal
    The Right Market for You

The Local Market

Innkeeping Seminars

To Build or to Buy, and Why?

Buying an Existing Inn
    Shopping for a Country Inn

Creating Your Own Inn
    Starting from Scratch
    Inspection
    Local Building Codes

How Big is Big Enough?

The Destination Inn
    Location Location Location

The Inngoer
    What Brings You to Town?

The Inn and the Community
    Creating Your Own Niche in the Community
    Why Isn't Everyone Smiling?

Professionalism

Market Positioning
    Marketing Today . . . for Tomorrow

Y ou can never know too much about the market you propose to
enter. A firm grasp of the demographics of the people you plan
to serve, paired with a clear understanding of the place where
you wish to locate your country inn, will provide the objective foundation necessary for rational decision making.

> "When I suggested to Louise that it might be fun to open a B&B
> or a small inn, we disciplined ourselves to apply some common
> sense logic to the proposition. How much could we afford? Where?
> How? Santa Fe as a location was a sound business decision. It is
> a terrific year-round destination.
> "It is a wonderful way of life, but it is still a business. You still
> have a family to support, and the need for the basic necessities of
> life. So don't forget to give sober consideration to what kind of
> business you are getting into. Most new innkeepers never mention
> they are getting into the business to make a living. It's always 'Isn't
> this a wonderful way of life' or 'Don't you just love meeting people?'"

THE LODGING MARKET

Analyzing your market begins by familiarizing yourself with the work
already done by others. Since inngoers are a subset of the broader
travel and tourism market, it will be instructive for you to research the
overall lodging market first. As you do so, however, keep in mind the
important demographic differences between travelers who visit standard hotels and those who prefer inns. These differences will weigh
heavily on your marketing and strategic planning.

The typical hotel guest has less education (40 percent of all hotel
guests have undergraduate or graduate college degrees, vs. 70 percent
of inn guests), less annual income (38 percent of all hotel guests have
annual incomes of $50,000 or more, vs. 54 percent of inn guests), and is
older (mean age: forty-five) than the inn guest (mean age: forty).

With more than 45,020 properties offering in excess of three million guest rooms, generating 61 billion dollars in sales annually, the task
of analyzing the industry can be formidable. Fortunately, much of the
tedious research has already been done for you.

Standard Rate & Data Service (3004 Glenview Road, Wilmette, IL
60091) publishes the *SRDS Media & Market Planner for Travel and
Tourism Markets*. This 340-page $149 resource is a comprehensive
introduction to the travel market in general, and the lodging market in
particular, and should be available in your local library. Pay particularly

close attention to how the top 100 lodging markets are analyzed. You'll quickly see that the lodging business revolves around a tight core of three important variables.

1. Occupancy Percentage — Percentage sold of available guest rooms.

2. Percent Change in Occupancy compared to last year for the same period.

3. Average Room Rate charged.

These three variables will help you begin getting an overall sense of the market in your own geographic area.

Not All Markets Are Created Equal

As you will quickly observe as you begin familiarizing yourself with the lodging market, some areas are more attractive for the development of a country inn than others. For example, the occupancy percentage of all hotel rooms in the twenty-five largest metropolitan areas in 1991 varied from 50.9 percent in Detroit to 75.3 percent in Las Vegas. Average room rates varied even more dramatically, from a low of $46.61 in Las Vegas to New York's average rate of $116.53. Perhaps not surprisingly, based upon the overall condition of the U.S. economy, both New York and Las Vegas showed declines in occupancy and average rates when compared to the same period in 1990.

Although these figures might appear to be irrelevant to the market for your country inn, the form of the analysis certainly is not. As a prospective innkeeper, you should analyze your prospective market in much the same manner as SRDS analyzes the top lodging markets in the nation. The occupancy rates, changes in occupancy rates year to year, and the room rates of lodging facilities in your market constitute the first essential elements in your own objective market analysis.

Among the data covered in the SRDS materials, you will also find a state-by-state comparison of rates and occupancy levels, which point up dramatic differences among states and regions. Although these surveys and reports are interesting as basic generic research, no isolated survey should be used as the "stand alone" rationale for determining the one best market for your new country inn. For example, based strictly upon the change in occupancy levels from 1990 to 1991, Delaware and North Dakota would appear to be the most positive lodging markets in the United States. But before you quit your day job, put in your change of address slips, and begin having your mail forwarded to either state, it is important to consider a few other variables — not the least of which is where you want to live!

The Right Market For You

At the risk of sounding overly simplistic, the most important first step in picking the right market for your country inn is to pick a part of the country you know you like. If you've spent your life in the South, and you love it, it would not be a good idea to select an inn opportunity in the Pacific Northwest, Delaware, or North Dakota, no matter how good a deal it might be, or how "hot" the lodging market might appear.

Don't overlook the other "specs" you and your partner feel are important to maintaining your lifestyle and your well-being. If you consider a world-class symphony and important art gallery essential to a well-rounded existence, then identify the orchestras and galleries that meet your criteria and locate them on a map. Next, identify the outer limits of your driving tolerance — say three hours — and concentrate your inn market search within those boundaries.

On a less esoteric level, locating near — or not so near, as the case may be — other family members, the mountains, the ocean, the desert, the dry air, the moist heat, etc., can all play a part in narrowing your search.

Once you've found a region that matches most if not all of your personal criteria, you can focus your research on the country inn opportunities that might exist in that specific area.

THE LOCAL MARKET

You will be pleasantly surprised to discover how much local market information already exists free of charge, if you know where to look for it. Start with the Chamber of Commerce, the economic development office, and the Yellow Pages. A wealth of information is available within each, from community concerns to possible competitors, from traffic patterns to available properties.

Since you are about to enter the lodging, food, and beverage business, learn all you can about those businesses in your town. Collect their literature and patronize them to get a first-hand look at what they do well and not so well, and why. Subscribe to the newspaper and pay particular attention to the advertising. Who advertises most? Least? Or not at all? Start a collection of ads in each major category you plan to serve. Keep your eyes open for the peripheral businesses that exist on the fringe of each category, such as catering, party planning, and travel agencies.

What types of "specials" appear regularly? It's a good bet that if you see numerous "buy one-get one" hospitality deals, you're looking at a soft market. The same thing holds true for the hotels, motels, inns, and resorts in your area. If the lodging community in your market is hungry for business and heavily emphasizing pricing in their advertising, look closer to determine whether this market can even support the country inn you are planning to open. As you collect your information on the advertising going on *now*, do not overlook the fact that your area might be a seasonal market with traffic and promotion patterns that reflect the high and low seasons. As part of getting to know your market better, make certain you are able to identify the natural flow of business and that your financial projections reflect those expectations.

The tax office can provide you with census data by zip code that will provide you with a "lay of the land" relative to your local potential clientele. Since most of your business will be drawn from out-of-town visitors, you'll want to expand your market analysis to include the region surrounding your own community. Consider carefully how your target guest will get to your location. Are you near an interstate highway? Will most of your guests arrive by air? Once you've determined the primary mode of transportation for your arriving guest, you can then take steps to intersect your potential customer at the opportune and most cost-effective time and place.

Before taking the plunge, it is instructive to consider the quantity and quality of research done by some of America's most successful country innkeepers before and after they entered the business. Ironically, the ones who have been in business the longest very often did the least amount of research. Why? Because they were dealing with an entirely different market in every respect. The explosion in the innkeeping industry in the past decade has translated to a more crowded and competitive environment. In addition, more demanding financial institutions insist on fully developed marketing plans and feasibility studies. This has improved both the quality and the quantity of the market research being done today in conjunction with the opening of country inns.

The roundtable members felt, and mentioned consistently, that market research involves basic common sense thinking. Regardless of how formal your own market research might be, the most valuable primary market research you conduct will undoubtedly consist of staying in inns in the area. Along the way, you'll pick up a number of excellent ideas that can be adapted and put to work in your inn.

Maybe even more importantly, you'll also be able to pick out a lot of the things you do not want to incorporate into your operation. Your selection of those concepts you like will result in the touches and policies that, combined with your own personality, create a country inn that bears your own unique imprint.

INNKEEPING SEMINARS

Not a month goes by without an inn seminar taking place some-where in the United States, and if there's not one near you now, there soon will be. In fact, seminars for prospective innkeepers are now available afloat, as part of work/play vacations on some cruise ships.

If your tastes run more towards staying inland, the longest- running continuing "road-show" for prospective innkeepers is still at it, after more than a decade of doing what they do best:

Oates & Bredfeldt (P.O. Box 1162, Brattleboro, VT 05302, 802-254-5931) are the leading consultants in the field. Throughout your discussions with innkeepers, you will be intrigued by how often the name Bill Oates comes up. You will quickly learn why. It's hard not to respect a consultant who will tell you without a blink that talking some-one out of a career in innkeeping might very well be the greatest ser-vice he can pay that person and the industry. When someone attends an Oates & Bredfeldt Seminar and chooses not to enter the business, Bill feels that he has helped that person understand the reality of innkeeping, *and* helped the industry avoid an unsuccessful attempt at running a country inn.

> According to Bill Oates, his chosen lot in life is helping people avoid the mistake of pouring their life savings — not to mention those precious years when they actually have a choice about what to do with their lives — into a dream career that can quickly become a nightmare.

In addition to the Oates & Bredfeldt programs, **Innkeeping Con-sultants** (P.O. Box 79, Okemos, MI 48805, 1-800-926-4667) and Carl Glassman's **Wedgwood Inn School** (111 West Bridge Street, New Hope, PA 18938, 1-215-862-2570) both offer periodic seminars of varying lengths that cover everything from bookkeeping to tea service, and quite a lot in between. If neither offers a program that is right for you, ask them about other seminars they know about. You'll find innkeepers and those who train aspiring professionals to be very forthcoming about what's available, by whom, where, and when.

TO BUILD OR BUY, AND WHY?

With or without the benefit of one of the innkeeping seminars, you should begin now to determine whether you prefer to purchase an existing country inn or create one. As you will see, there are pros and cons for either choice.

Ten years ago this section of *How to Open and Successfully Operate a Country Inn* would not have been necessary. The pioneers of the industry who began their operations then had only one choice. Too few inns existed for there to be a real market of inn properties. As a result, if you entered the business before the mid-1980s, you would have located an appropriate real estate opportunity and started from scratch with an inn of your own creation.

The primary differences between buying and creating a country inn lie in the initial application of development funds. If you acquire an existing business, you quite naturally will be paying the seller for such intangibles as good will, along with important tangible leasehold improvements such as a commercial kitchen and six or seven private baths. On the other hand, if you are planning to convert an existing structure to an inn, you will probably pay less initially for the property — and considerably more to upfit the building to serve as a country inn.

BUYING AN EXISTING INN

When you purchase an existing inn:

- You generally pay more money than you would in a straight real estate acquisition.
- You buy a facility already staffed and adapted for the lodging and hospitality requirements of a country inn.
- You acquire the existing identity (good or bad), good will (positive or negative), name, and reputation of an already up-and-running business.
- If you've done your homework and ensured the inn's compliance with all existing health, safety, and zoning ordinances, you can focus immediately on marketing.
- You acquire the inn's customer list.

There are certain distinct advantages to purchasing an existing inn. But take a moment to review the operating history of the property you are considering for acquisition. Is the track record consistently positive? Do sales and gross profits trend upward? If the business appears to have peaked and is in decline, it might be a great time for the seller to sell but not a particularly good time for you to buy. As you review the list above, keep in mind that the most important information available to you is the inn's own operating statement.

Shopping for a Country Inn

The explosion in the number of country inns and bed and breakfasts across the nation in the past ten years has resulted in a phenomenal increase in the number of inn properties for sale at any given time. In order to serve the industry better, several publications now regularly feature a section on inns for sale, and a number of business brokers have begun specializing in the industry.

Innkeeping, the monthly newsletter of the Professional Association of Innkeepers International (805-569-1853), *Inn Business Review* (815-939-3509), and *The Inn Broker, Inc.* (800-926-4667) all regularly publish an up-to-date list of inns on the market. There are other regional publications and a broad range of business and real estate brokerage firms that might also be able to provide you with information on available properties in the area you have chosen as your target marketplace.

Just because an inn is not "on the market" does not mean that it is not for sale. As the old adage goes, "everything is for sale — at a price." If you are reluctant to approach an owner innkeeper directly, then have an intermediary test the waters on your behalf. Many business owners (innkeepers included) consider a serious, discreet inquiry into the possibility of purchasing their business to be a distinct form of high praise. In any event, you never know what might be for sale until you ask.

Whether the huge rise in available properties has resulted from overeager first-timers, early burnouts, or simply folks who are ready to move on to the next chapter in their own lives, the end result is the same: it's an excellent time to be shopping around for a country inn. Given the current favorable market for acquiring an existing inn, and the extraordinarily high cost of creating a new one, it would make sense to review the inventory of properties on the market — if for no other reason than to gain a better understanding of the business.

If you've not already shopped around, you might find the following selected sample of inns recently sold in the United States to be of interest. As you will observe, the comparison "price per guest room" for the ongoing inns in this sample varies considerably from $52,084 for a twelve-bedroom North Carolina in-town inn to $170,833 for a nineteen-bedroom New York coastal village inn with a good occupancy ratio. The price per guest room will of course vary widely depending upon the operating history of the inn, its location, and its condition.

Selected Sample of Inn Sales

Location Attraction	Type of Property Guestrooms/Baths	Sale Date Price	Comparison Indices*		Commentary
			Price per Guestroom	GRM OAR	
Washington State-Rural	Victorian Farmhouse 8/6	1992 $440,000	$55,000	6.3 6%	Coastal area. 8 years in operation. Low occupancy ratio, poor management.
Napa Valley California	Modern Replica 16/16	1991 $1,085,000	$67,812	4.5 10.1%	"New England Rustic," 5 years in business.
Calistoga Hot Springs California	Historic House 6/6	1991 $670,000	$111,667	4.2 11%	Well seasoned business Destination village.
Virginia rurual	Farmhouse 7/7 + 68 seat restaurant	1992 $825,000	$117,857	1.45 12.1%	Well seasoned operation 23% of revenue from inn, 77% food and bev.
New York Coastal Village	Vintage 19/19 + 70-seat restaurant and bar	1992 $1,050,000	$170,833	1.2 12%	Established 12-year operation, good occup. ratio.
North Carolina In-town	Vintage Inn 12/12 + 48-seat restaurant	1992 $615,000	$51,084	4.3 10%	In operation as inn for over 80 years.
Vermont Village	Historic Inn 29/29 + pub and restaurant	1993 $2,700,000	$93,103	1.5 14.0%	Full-service inn. Good operating history. 26% of revenue from inn, 74% food and bev.

KEY: Comparison Indices include all operating business assets, real and personal property, intangible business assets including good will, if any.

Price per guestroom: total purchase price divided by number of guest units.
    GRM: the total purchase price as a multiple of the annual gross revenue.
    OAR: the overall rate of return or "capitalization rate," being the net annual operating income as a percentage retun on the total investment.

Prepared by G. Michael Yovino-Young, SREA, SRA, ASA   June 1993
    Yovino-Young, Incorporated, Berkeley California   Reproduced by permission

CREATING YOUR OWN INN

When you purchase a suitable building for conversion to a country inn:

- You generally pay less money for the structure and/or the land than you would if it were already up and running as a country inn.
- You generally pay considerably more money on the leasehold improvements necessary to bring your property up to code and to open the facility as a country inn.
- You design and decorate your new facility to your own tastes and the tastes of the guests you plan to serve.
- You determine the name, theme, and identity of the property.
- You start from scratch, with all the joy and heartaches that go along with starting any business.

Starting from Scratch

Since totally new construction is a rare phenomenon in this industry (generally limited to larger resort hotels), most "from scratch" startups begin with an appealing building in a good location, which is then retrofitted for life as an inn.

The Innkeepers' Roundtable (see Introduction) is an excellent cross-section of successful innkeepers within the industry, and as such, it is revealing to point out that only one roundtable member purchased an existing inn when they entered the business. Other than Judd and Susan Levy's Vermont Inn, every other roundtable member found their building first and upfitted it for operation as a country inn. Nevertheless, here's how one roundtable member feels about startups:

"If I had it to do over again, I would not, under any circumstances, start an inn from scratch again. We love our part of the country and we wanted to stay here, so when we decided to tackle the inn business, we really had no choice. There were no viable country inns in our immediate area, so we decided to create one. If we were ever going to reenter the business I can assure you we would do so by purchasing an existing operation. Starting from scratch is so very difficult. Just getting the word out through the media that you exist can be a daunting full-time task."

There are circumstances where starting from scratch as a country inn in an ideal location might make good business sense. Certainly Pat

Walters and Louise Stewart felt that was the case when they acquired the old frame house in Santa Fe that they converted to an inn. The Grant Corner Inn is a professional and personal success, primarily because of the decision made by the innkeepers to invest the extra money for a prime Santa Fe location two blocks from the square. *"It was without a doubt our smartest investment,"* says Pat. That decision has translated to a country inn that stays fully booked many months of the year, and often must turn guests away. Pat and Louise decided to spend the money to be located where people wanted to be first — and to create a warm and hospitable inn to serve them second.

The Henry F. Shaffner House in Winston-Salem, North Carolina, is another example of a location ideally suited for life as an inn. Located three blocks from the heart of the central business district, this historically significant old homeplace is situated between most of the major corporate offices in the community and the highest-occupancy moderately upscale hotel in town. In addition, unlike many communities its size, Winston-Salem was noticeably "underbuilt" in the inn category of lodging facilities. The attractive initial acquisition cost, proximity to business traffic, ease of access, and a proven demand for overnight lodging in the price range offered by the inn combined to make this startup a viable choice for the innkeepers. There are indeed certain compelling advantages to the scratch startup.

Inspection

Restoration/renovation of an existing structure with the potential of being a country inn might be a cost-effective way for you to enter the business. Please notice the word "might." If you have fallen in love with a building that you believe could be reborn as the greatest country inn in history — STOP. Step back from the romance long enough to bring in an architect or builder who is trained to conduct a full inspection of the physical structure.

The object of your affection might turn out to be in immediate (and costly) need of a new heating system (and it probably is), a new roof (and it probably is), rewiring (and — you get the picture). Whether you plan to renovate, restore, remodel, or some clever budget-busting combination of all three, you must bring in a disinterested third party to inspect your property from the footings to the weathervane, in order to avoid the disastrous mistake of buying the proverbial money pit.

In your travels around country inns, be sure to include questions about the innkeeper's first-hand knowledge of money pits. Their stories will entertain and inform . . . and with a little luck perhaps keep you from joining the ranks of other lovers of wonderful old buildings whose love, in the clear light of day, faded to loathing.

Local Building Codes

Second-guessing the local building codes, zoning ordinances, and health and safety regulations is a potentially disastrous mistake. Every community in America has a different set of codes and regulations this year than they had last year, and it is a safe bet they'll be different next year than they are today. Make certain that the building you plan to remodel or acquire can indeed be operated as a country inn. That might mean that you need to retain local counsel to sort through the regulations, but it will be money well spent. That same counsel could come in quite handy if you need to seek a variance that permits you to operate without strict adherence to existing ordinances.

Even with the appropriate licenses and permits in place at the time of the acquisition, local or state health and safety authorities can still enter your place of business within days of your purchase and mandate extensive and costly modifications to your operation. One way to avoid this is to require a complete health and safety inspection report as a condition of the closing. Making certain the inn meets current health and safety codes and regulations is every bit as important as a current termite inspection; neglecting it at the time of purchase can be every bit as costly. If for any reason the property fails to pass inspection subsequent to the sale, the seller should be held financially responsible for bringing it into compliance.

In some communities, particularly if the idea of a country inn is a new concept to city officials, it is possible that no specific rules, regulations, or ordinances cover the operation of your business. In this case, you have an excellent opportunity to become the resident authority on country inns and the ordinances governing them. Contact the national and regional innkeeping associations and assemble a package of information on how other communities handle the rules governing inns. By volunteering to help in the early stages you avoid the possibility of developing an adversarial relationship at the outset. You have become an insider before you even open the door.

HOW BIG IS BIG ENOUGH?

Why Have More Guest Rooms?
When demand warrants, more rooms mean greater gross revenue. More revenue means the ability to hire more and better-trained staff to perform the duties that might otherwise have to be assumed by the innkeeper.

Whether you decide to start from scratch or buy an existing inn, it is a good idea to determine early on the size of property that best suits your own personality, temperament, skills, goals, and budget. As one authority on country inn development has said, in innkeeping, less is definitely MORE. In a small inn of fewer than eight guest rooms, the owner/innkeeper does more of everything. If you are a "hands-on" type manager with a jack-of-all-trades philosophy, a small inn might be right up your alley.

If, on the other hand, you would prefer to hire someone to handle the housekeeping and/or building maintenance, then a larger facility would permit you to generate the necessary volume of sales to support the added cost of additional staff support. The other half of the corollary is equally true — more (as in number of guest rooms) is going to mean LESS direct innkeeper/owner involvement in the day-to-day chores of running the inn.

There is nothing more critical to your success than the number of guest rooms you have at your inn. Too many or too few guest rooms can spell financial disaster. Supplying the appropriate number of guest rooms to meet the current and future demands of your market will move you toward early and lasting profitability. Early in the research for this book, it was striking how many successful innkeepers commented that, if they had it to do over again, they would have had more guest rooms — and the accompanying increase in gross revenues those rooms would represent.

On the other hand, don't rush to buy more rooms than you can fill at first, simply because you hope you will need them later. An excess inventory of unused rooms is almost always fatal. Even well-financed new innkeepers who have been extremely conservative with their worst- and best-case marketing scenarios cannot survive extended periods of debt servicing on under-utilized square footage.

As one roundtable member put it:

"Now that we're on the happy (and profitable) side of ten years of

innkeeping we really have only one regret. We purchased an inn with only eight guest rooms, and one that is not easily expanded architecturally. You know what they say about 20/20 hindsight.

"In retrospect it would have been great over the past few high seasons to have had six or eight more revenue-generating guest rooms and a few more full tables in our dining room. But in order to have that we would have had to trade considerable peace of mind in our early seasons in the business — and there probably would have been no shortage of sleepless nights while we established ourselves."

Now, after a decade of success, this couple feels that if they ever bought another property, it would be one with more guest rooms and higher potential gross sales.

THE DESTINATION INN

Much of this discussion has presupposed that you are planning to acquire or locate your new country inn in an area where a market of some kind has already been established. If you have found the "perfect" location for your dream country inn and it just happens to be well off the beaten path, then your marketing challenges will be dramatically more significant. You are planning to open what is euphemistically referred to as a "destination inn."

As the name implies, a "destination" inn is a facility that is its own best — and often only — draw or attraction. Before you write the down payment check for your very own destination property, you might want to pay close attention to the comments of innkeepers who have had their own first-hand experiences with operating this type of establishment.

As one innkeeper explained, *"Midweek was always a major challenge, and I believe that was a direct result of our location."* In the inn business, a destination property almost always enjoys "full house" weekends and slow or nonexistent midweek traffic. Therefore, the innkeepers who operate a destination inn must be adept at promoting their property midweek, in order to fill in the gap. Inns located in or near an urban center have a much easier time attracting the midweek traveling business traffic that is often the key to ongoing profitability.

As Pat Walter says, *"I tell people you can find beautiful buildings all over the country, but if you're going to end up spending all your time and money selling visitors on your area, I'm not sure you're making the right business decision."* The consensus among the round-table members was that the business of innkeeping was a big enough challenge without the burden of a poor location.

There are certainly examples of marvelous facilities that have evolved into a destination in their own right. Louise Stewart's father, in fact, developed one of the world's finest destination resorts — from literally nothing but open arid desert land.

The Camelback Inn has become an incredible success story, leading the thriving Paradise Valley/Scottsdale, Arizona, tourism market for many years. As a prospective country innkeeper, however, you might look at several of the factors that were fundamental to the success of Camelback. First, the developer was a highly skilled marketing professional with a flair for entrepreneurial creativity. Second, he had sufficient financial strength to wait from 1936, when he began construction, for his marketing programs to succeed. The facility was acquired by Marriott in 1967 and has grown today to the status of a world-class 423-room resort.

You get the picture. Entrepreneurial genius, financial staying power, and patience are as important as the bricks and mortar in a facility that strives to operate as a destination in its own right. Concentrate your market research on areas that have already proven their ability to attract a crowd, and then you'll be able to shift marketing emphasis to focus specifically on the primary competition in your target market.

Location Location Location

In real estate evaluation the top three components of value are location, location, and location. The same basic philosophy holds true in determining the relative value of a country inn. Successful country innkeepers can be generally grouped into one of two categories: those whose location is the primary reason for their success; and those who have overcome their poor location and succeeded through creativity and perseverance.

Mark Carter's Carter House might be considered somewhat out of the way. Located in Eureka, California, five hours north of San Francisco, and eight hours south of Portland, Oregon, the Carter House has had to develop a substantial part of its business from the tour groups that travel through the area on the way to see the giant redwoods and other scenic attractions of the Pacific Northwest. Recognizing the need to tap into that market segment, the Carters have cultivated a close relationship with all the tour operations and constantly keep them up to date on the Carter House facilities. Ask Mark how location has affected his business and he will quickly tell you, *"If I could pick up our inn and move it closer to the San Francisco Bay area, we would probably be full all the time. As a result of our location, we've had to be very creative and aggressive about promoting ourselves."*

When asked to consider which lessons he would apply to another country inn operation, Mark candidly admits, *"If I were to develop another property, we would locate closer to a more substantial population center to increase guest counts throughout the week."*

On the opposite extreme of the destination inn is the inn located in the heart of a destination community. If your entire neighborhood happens to be listed in the National Registry of Historic Places . . . so much the better. For Hugh and Roberta Lineberger, their instinct for going into the inn business in Savannah, Georgia, was right on target.

The Linebergers came to Savannah on a Sunday to play golf at Hilton Head and fell head over heels in love with the town. Five days later they bought the two adjoining homes that now constitute the Gastonian. When you talk about "market" with Hugh, he quickly points to one vital component for their success. *"I think we owe a lot of our success — maybe even most — to the fact that we are located in the heart of the largest historic landmark district in the United States."*

According to the Savannah Chamber of Commerce, the Number One business in Savannah is the military, followed closely by tourism. Visitors come to Savannah for the world-famous sights of this historic Southern town, often without prior knowledge of any inn. The Gastonian, therefore, considers its challenge to be attracting their share of the visitors to the community rather than attracting the visitors to town in the first place. Accordingly, the only regular advertising the Gastonian buys is a display ad in the local Chamber of Commerce's visitor guidebook.

Since Hugh considers his location so fundamental to his success, we asked if he thought it was possible to overcome a less-than-desirable location. *"If you have this wonderful gorgeous home out in the middle of nowhere, one of your first decisions has to be how you are going to attract people to your inn. As you ponder that question, you need to remember to budget two things: money to advertise . . . a lot; and time to await the results. Both money and time are precious commodities to a new innkeeper."*

> Despite our urging that prospective innkeepers must do their homework there are those dreamers who bought first and analyzed later. On occasion they even succeed. One such example would have to be the Linebergers and their remarkably successful Gastonian.

When Hugh and Roberta began the inn, they were like a lot of other innkeepers — somewhat unsophisticated about their potential market. Both admit that they didn't identify their target market, it identified them. Since the Gastonian is a thirteen-room double occupancy inn, their primary market is couples, and their secondary market, single travelers. The Linebergers candidly admit they were fortunate to be in a market with sufficient tourist traffic to support them while they found their way to their own target base market.

It is interesting to note that some innkeepers, certainly a minority, do not readily agree that location is the single most important element in the successful marketing of a country inn. Deedy and Charlie Marble are among this group. Sure, they agree, it helps to be in the perfect high-visibility high-traffic spot — but it is certainly not a prerequisite.

As concrete evidence of their theory, the Marbles are justifiably proud that they serve roughly the same number of guests each year in their small inn as the entire permanent population of their community, Ludlow, Vermont. Clearly, the Marbles have been successful at attracting a lot of folks to a somewhat out-of-the-way location.

It should also be pointed out that even the Governor's Inn has profited by the success of those around them. Through the bedroom window upstairs that faces north and west you have a clear view of one of Vermont's most thriving ski resorts — Okemo Mountain. The success of the resort as a destination location has been an important ancillary marketing draw for the little Inn in Ludlow.

Now that you have narrowed your search down to one or two places that fit your personal needs and marketing goals, it's time to look at the person you plan to target — the human side of your primary market.

THE INNGOER

Several recent surveys of inngoers have revealed that the inn experience is still a special occasion, with the majority of visitors making inns part of their pleasure travel away from home only once or twice over the course of an eighteen-month period. Once at the inn, the guest will generally spend two or three nights at somewhere between $75 and $125 per night. In many ways the typical inn guest is a marketer's dream come true. According to the Professional Association of Innkeepers International, more than 54 percent of the people who visit inns have household incomes in excess of $50,000, and 89 percent of them have attended college. The inngoer is generally married and between the ages of twenty-five and fifty-four.

When your target customers arrive at your door, don't be surprised to meet them two at a time — 70 percent of inn guests travel as couples. Since the overwhelming majority of inngoers found their inn in a guidebook or learned about it from a friend or relative, two important components of your marketing strategy have already been identified for you.

The inngoer knows exactly which characteristics of an inn experience will encourage their return and which will not. The warmth and hospitality of the innkeeper lead the list of elements guests considered most conducive to another visit, followed closely by a private bath and memorable food. Number One on the list of inn turnoffs was lack of cleanliness — ironically, an absolutely controllable part of the business. Not surprisingly, poor food, slow service, and indifferent inn staff were also considered key reasons not to return.

What Brings You to Town?

Understanding the human side of the marketing equation must begin with analyzing not only who your guest is, but also what brings him or her to your door in the first place. Depending on your location, your typical guest might be visiting your area on business, on vacation, or just stopping in on the way somewhere else.

To Play

Clearly, the Number One reason people visit and stay overnight in an area 100 miles or more away from home is recreation. "Ski Country," for example, is home to some of the finest country inns in America. Those inns have learned how to attract the sports enthusiast. For example, folks who bicycle across Vermont or spend ten hours a day on the ski slopes are generally in better-than-average physical condition — and somewhat more health-conscious than the general public.

Special high-energy meals for people who burn up megacalories are just one way to cater to that public; there are plenty of other things you can do to get a "leg up" on your competition. You wouldn't typically expect to find a massage therapist, for example, with his own portable massage table, at a country inn — unless, of course, it is the Inn at Weathersfield in Vermont, hosting a tour group of exhausted and sore bicyclists. Suddenly this extra touch makes enormous good sense.

Even the physical layout of your inn can be thoughtfully designed to accommodate the unique needs of the market you plan to serve. This means, for example, having a mudroom for skiers and hikers if you don't wish to replace the foyer carpeting every other year.

There are dozens of subset markets available to the highly focused, market-sensitive country innkeeper. Whether it's butterfly collectors, fishermen, mountain climbers, aspiring gold prospectors, or spelunkers, you must make it your business to understand their interests and unique lodging and hospitality requirements. Subscribe to the magazines that serve their interests . . . speak with them . . . serve them.

To Work

In recent years, people whose jobs mandate travel have begun to discover the country inn alternative for lodging. If you are located in or near the mainstream of commerce in your area, chances are you're in a position to attract the frequent traveler. Like every other segment of the inngoing public, the business traveler has a particular group of needs that must be addressed if you want to attract his or her repeat business. Fax machines, convenient telephones or, better still, jacks or remote telephones in the room are all comparatively lowcost amenities that could appeal to your business market.

Several third-party telephone service suppliers market a special telephone setup for inn guests that permits the innkeeper to collect a small service fee on each call. If the business traveler is high on your prospective-client list, you would be well advised to make long-distance telephone service easily accessible and reasonably priced. Since many "business" hotel chains now make it a policy to tack on a flat charge even for credit card non-operator-assisted calls, here is an opportunity to differentiate your inn by refusing to "up-charge" your guest.

Establish a close working relationship with the businesses in your area — perhaps by dropping off some brochures and a basket of fresh-baked muffins with the receptionist. This will help them remember your inn as a lodging alternative for their out-of-town business guests.

One cautionary note here: since country inns are primarily sought out as a refuge from the world of business, be discreet when offering the business amenities to those who need and appreciate them, so as not to intrude upon the guest who prefers quiet solitude. It is possible to serve both clients without turning off either one.

To Stay

Many successful country inns have located in or near popular retirement communities. If that is your choice, market sensitivity will again be crucial to your long-term success. Since retirement developments cater to a constantly growing market, make it known to the community that you welcome and can cater to those who visit as part of their plans to relocate to the area. Older, less active inn guests may be physically challenged by steep multi-flight stairways and appreciate ground-floor accommodations. Diets lower in fat and sodium have now become the standard for all health-conscious Americans, but particularly so with the older traveling public.

THE INN AND THE COMMUNITY

Now that you know a little more about the inngoer and the variety of reasons he or she might choose to visit, let's move on to a more specific discussion of the market you plan to serve.

Early in their innkeeping experience Pat and Louise learned that even in an internationally known tourist destination like Santa Fe, you simply cannot survive in the inn business on tourism alone. Pat emphasizes that lesson by pointing out that, *"Your local community will be there with you day in and day out . . . regardless of the season."*

Community involvement is critical to the role country innkeepers play in their primary marketplace. Perhaps surprisingly, innkeepers often wear a lot of different hats in their communities. One roundtable participant mentioned he was particularly proud of the role he played in the design, funding, and construction of his town's new seven-million-dollar sewer system. When you look closer at this particular community, you realize that the innkeeper's involvement in improving the way his town handles its effluent is close to the heart of his business. The tributaries into which the waste is discharged meander through the inn's own back yard and provide important scenic and recreational opportunities for inn guests.

Overwhelmingly, successful players in this segment of the hospitality industry consider themselves to be partners in the business community — and they commit their time and money accordingly. A high profile in community affairs lends a definite legitimacy to the new country inn in town. By embracing the community, the innkeepers become insiders themselves, resulting ultimately in the new inn being accepted by the neighborhood.

Creating Your Own Niche in the Community

With minimal cost and inconvenience, the inn can become the social focus of important local groups and organizations. Create a market for yourself by targeting those smaller groups who meet at midday, when you are normally not serving guests. Offer the inn for functions that can be served by your kitchen and lodging facilities.

> The Clifton Inn in Charlottesville has too few guest rooms to accommodate most wedding parties, so they have cleverly carved out a market niche of their own. They specialize in serving the bride's family. This works out beautifully for the eight or ten couples who constitute the bridal party, and it works out nicely for the inn as well.

Once the word is out that you are flexible and willing to work with groups of all sizes, the businesses in town will begin using the inn for meetings and special functions. It is just a matter of time until the same people begin to think of your inn as the ideal home away from home for their own out-of-town guests.

Why Isn't Everyone Smiling?

Once the hard decisions are made and the finances arranged, it is perhaps difficult to understand why every member of the local business community may not be uniformly positive and enthusiastic about your country inn. The misconceptions about country innkeeping are the subject of a lot of innkeeper frustration.

The smaller the town, and the fewer the number of successful inn properties, the greater the possibility the new innkeeper will encounter some resistance from the local business community. Since very often the new country inn will be occupying one of the more venerable structures in the community, some townspeople may argue that an inn is not worthy of the space. Others, with little or no knowledge of first-class country inns, will seek to hold the inn to the same operational standards as the local Holiday Inn. *"After all, they're both inns, aren't they?"*

B&Bs, on the other hand, are variously interpreted as houses of ill repute, lodgings on the edge, boarding houses, etc. This becomes yet another challenge for the country innkeeper.

Depending on the flow of out-of-towners and vacationers in the area, acceptance by the local community may not be a prerequisite to the ultimate success of the business. However, getting along with the local business community will make the day-to-day life of the innkeeper considerably more pleasant. As one of the roundtable members explained, *"Once we held our Christmas open house for the Garden Club and announced that we had successfully added our trees to the Historic Registry, the trivial social barriers began to fall and we slowly grew to be accepted as a member of the community."*

If your inn is successful it will probably be held in high regard by the community, which will indirectly prosper when you prosper. It is naive to assume, however, that all members of the competitive retail environment and/or other innkeepers will be uniformly thrilled by your success. In the final analysis, the degree of acceptance by the local community will be measured more in terms of results and less in terms of the emotions.

PROFESSIONALISM

The innkeeping industry has undergone some interesting changes over the past decade. In the early days of innkeeping, for example, people accepted the European standard of shared baths. With an increasingly competitive inn environment, private baths have become the mandate. Guests expect more luxury today. That cute, modest country inn has been replaced by a broader array of innkeeping amenities and more luxurious facilities.

According to one successful Southwestern innkeeper, *"It seems the public really treasures and appreciates thoughtful and historically accurate renovation and furnishings — all the way to the bathroom door. Once they hit the bathroom they're ready to immediately swap quaint and fashionable antiquity for Jacuzzis, bidets, and gold-plated high-pressure pulsating showers."*

The biggest change in the industry over the past ten years is the positive move toward increased professionalism. This truly distinguishes the operators of country inns from the bed and breakfast and homestay operators. Even though innkeepers like to say that their business is really a lifestyle, it is also important to point out that each successful operator interviewed for this book also emphasized the business side of innkeeping.

Even the innkeepers with superb markets, and ideal locations within those markets, were eager to emphasize that the location attracted a guest the first time, and convenience may have played a role in the second visit. But the reason the inn was successful year in and year out was the repeat business. People return to a country inn for a variety of reasons, including the warmth and hospitality of the innkeepers, the quality of the food, cleanliness and comfort, but the most compelling reason to return is the value received for the money spent.

Notwithstanding the professional differences between country inns, B&Bs, and homestays, the main difference is that the country innkeeper is operating a full-time business primarily to serve someone else's needs.

> "Professional" should not be taken to mean impersonal. Professionalism has to do with the quality of overall hospitality and the standards of excellence maintained by the innkeepers.

As inns have come to be more in vogue, and changes have inevitably occurred, the industry has had some of its own growing pains. As the perception of the business opportunity of innkeeping has improved, inns with little or no direct innkeeper involvement have appeared on the scene. Time, and the ever more discerning tastes of the inn visitor, will be the judge of whether these hybrid types of operation will survive and prosper or fall by the wayside.

The days of "sell the house and transfer the equity to a little inn somewhere" have ceased to exist in the country inn business. The higher investments demanded at the entry level of the business have resulted in attracting prospective innkeepers who may have the money to invest but who, in many instances, have neither the time nor the inclination to roll up their sleeves and become an owner/operator. But as one roundtable member explained, when asked to reflect upon this, *"At the risk of sounding somewhat biased, I don't think I could ever encourage anyone to enter this business unless they plan to do it as a day-to-day, hands-on enterprise."*

MARKETING POSITIONING

"We choose to 'market' rather than advertise," explained a successful innkeeper when asked how she went about the process of developing an advertising program. By "marketing" this particular entrepreneur meant all the collateral public relations, promotional, and personal elements that go into stimulating public interest in the inn. She continued, *"It has been our experience that our prospective guests carefully read what is written about our inn, but they are likely to simply skim or skip the paid ads."* This revelation manifests itself in a number of ways in the day-to-day operation and promotion of the inn. *"Wherever we go, we don't miss an opportunity to 'toot our own horn.' When we are called on by travel writers and editors we try to go the extra mile to help them succeed in their jobs. Remember, when they win, you win!"*

One example of unpaid marketing exposure that is still paying off for this particular innkeeper was a story on cooking schools that appeared in a recent issue of *Bon Appétit* magazine. Her inn's cooking school was one of eight highlighted, only two of which were located in the United States. The telephone inquiries resulting from this little article have been, according to the innkeeper, *"absolutely astounding."*

An out-of-the-way inn can attract a regular and profitable flow of guests, depending on the marketing niche emphasis of the innkeepers themselves. *"We've found that people who visit inns generally visit a number of them each year,"* one innkeeper told us. Inngoers visit inns for separate and distinct reasons — the scenic vistas, the physical activities or sports, the food, or the personality of the innkeeper. Because each inn has something different to offer, the frequent inn visitor never tires of making the rounds, even to comparatively remote inns.

In order to communicate your own unique marketing niche to your prospective guest, you must first identify it in your own mind and heart (see Part Three). It can revolve around anything from your dedication to be the premiere restaurant facility in the area to the collection of butterflies that the Magnolia Place Inn in Savannah proudly displays in its parlor. If your doll collection is a source of personal delight, make it your theme. Children's toys, collectable first-edition books, antique serving pieces, even rabbits have all served as thematic anchors for inns. Once you have clearly identified your niche, the task of communicating that theme will be much simpler.

Proper positioning in the marketplace not only serves to give the inn an identity, but it also serves to insulate the inn somewhat from the ordinary swings of commerce. *"Because we are located in the country, we positioned our property to appeal to those who enjoyed nature and outdoor activities. It's amazing how many people we have hosted year in and year out, in good economic times and bad, who simply choose not to share with us their 'real life' professions. It's almost as though the inn is their island of serenity away from everything they associate with their working lives."*

Country inns are uniquely independent of the vagaries of economic swings, gas rationing, and the other bellwether events that can adversely impact other retail businesses. Because a country inn falls comfortably into the category of a "small indulgence," many people perceive it more as a restorative necessity than as an expensive "once in a lifetime" vacation. Some inns, which on a road map might look like poor locations, prove to be exceptional opportunities by virtue of the other activities, events, and venues surrounding the market. These can help develop the market focus of the property with the changes of the season. Such inns take great pride in serving multiple publics.

Due to its location near two fine ski areas, the Vermont Inn is a tourist-oriented operation that focuses primarily — but not exclusively — on serving the ski enthusiasts who visit the Killington area. Killington, the largest ski area in New England, is ten minutes from the front door of the inn. The Vermont Inn is five miles from the second largest city in the state, Rutland, a community of 30,000 permanent residents. The inn draws a considerable amount of evening dinner business from Rutland, which contributes to the overall financial health of the property.

The Vermont Inn has three distinct seasons, with three distinctly different demographic targets. The winter skiing trade is typified by a young sports enthusiast who visits the inn for two to three days. The summer tourist crowd is a substantially older, mostly retired clientele, generally staying at the inn for four to seven days. Summer visitors often make the inn their base while they venture out and around northern Vermont. Uncharacteristically for a country inn, the Vermont Inn has a tennis court and pool on the premises; therefore, the summer months also attract many families on vacation in the area.

Fall is the transition season for the Vermont Inn. Visitors travel great distances to visit the Northeast for a glimpse of the crimson, gold, and amber hues of autumn. The typical Vermont Inn visitor during this season is able to set his or her own schedule independent of school schedules. The business traveler with flexibility and the retiree thus constitute the majority of guests between the family summer months and the crisp thrill of the ski season.

Marketing Today . . . for Tomorrow

"It is amazing to us how often one of our guests points out all of the lovely old buildings around us that have been converted to inns. What makes our inn different is our imprint. We have put a lot of ourselves in this place — it would have been devastating if our guests did not appreciate our efforts."

"We always take a lot of pride in having our guests depart with a strong sense of value. We try to give them more than they pay for. We know we've succeeded when one of our departing guests takes the time to book their next stay before they leave. That's like giving a first grader a gold star! If they bring two or three other couples along when they return, we feel as if we've just hit a grand slam home run."

As these comments reveal, successful innkeepers have made an important discovery about one of the most important competitive advantages in the industry. Unlike many industries, in the hospitality industry you get a report card every day — whether you're operating a 1,000-room hotel, a 300-seat limited-menu specialty restaurant, or a ten-room country inn. You don't have to wait for an accountant's analysis in order to know how well, or how poorly, your property was received by the guest. This type of market instancy can be enormously depressing, or it can be the single most important weapon in your management arsenal.

By listening to both the spoken and unspoken messages being sent out by your guest, you can instantly identify those areas of your operation that need adjustment one way or the other. Since as much as 75 to 80 percent of your business in a country inn will be a direct result of word of mouth, quick decisive action to correct an operational flaw is an absolute necessity.

"We consider developing a long-term relationship with each of our guests to be part of our mission. It's our job to make certain every person who leaves here has an excuse to tell others about our inn. We know that the majority of our business is repeat business, and that the bulk of our first-time visitors are here because someone told them about us. We actually now have guests who are the off-

spring of our regular guests — so in that sense we're one of the few intergenerational inns in America."

Here's a story that illustrates how important this nurturing of regular guests and referrals can be. One of our roundtable innkeepers had as a guest several years ago a staff lawyer with the Anheuser Busch Company in St. Louis. As a result of his satisfaction with the hospitality of the inn through the years, he has been personally responsible for generating regular inn visits from twenty-three different St. Louis families — and this can be directly documented! *"It gives us an enormous sense of accomplishment to realize that St. Louis is home to several hundred of our regular visitors — all because we served one man and his wife the way we like to be served when we visit an inn."*

This story also illustrates the value of accurate record keeping, and the critical importance of devising a workable program for staying in touch with your market. A regular way to reward regular customers has become an integral part of marketing in the airline industry, and at least one credit card program has created a program of cash back in proportion to the gross charges. In a country inn, the rewards are of course considerably lower-key, but no less important to the recipient. Knowing the special dates in the lives of your best customers, as well as their favorite wine, mineral water, cocktail, or flower, can become a vital marketing platform for the astute country innkeeper.

The combination of discretionary income and more places to spend it inevitably result in a change in the public's perception of value. As that perception evolves, the successful country innkeeper can maintain a competitive edge by adhering to the basics of highly personalized service. *"We've tried to stay somewhat above the 'price war' mentality by staying clearly focused on our target customer and continually improving what we already do well. That's the best way we know to deepen and widen the niche we've found for our operation in the marketplace."*

What is the long-term marketing future for this business? In a word, superb. A certain percentage of the traveling public will always appreciate the value-added quality and comfort provided by a good full-service country inn dedicated to hospitality excellence and proud to acknowledge their guest by name. There is a growing niche for the individualized lodging experiences offered by country inns. It embraces quality, service, architecture, history, local color, and personalized attention to detail.

The guests of a country inn are often extremely well traveled and thus familiar with the role played by chain hotels in the lodging industry. They clearly understand the difference between a chain hotel "stay" and a country inn "experience." As our ever more mobile society grows less and less personal, the appeal of a country inn will increase. Country innkeepers must stay involved with their guests. If the inn is an honest portrayal of the innkeeper's personal style, the guests will know it, and the inn will be an unequivocal marketing success.

GERRY ARNOLD

If you enjoy serving others, you have one essential attribute of a good innkeeper. Above, owner Keith Marshall at Madewood Plantation, Napoleonville, Louisiana.

Chapter Three

KNOW YOURSELF

Innkeeper Personality Profile
The Innkeeper "A" List

Expectations and Reality

Being Yourself
Stage of Life
Need for Privacy
Tolerance
Lifestyle
Putting On a Happy Face

Innkeeping and Your Significant Other
Private Time
Togetherness

Burnout
Taking Care of Yourself
Signs of Impending Burnout
Ways to Avoid Burnout
Ways to Cut Down on Your Own Work

Rewards of the Lifestyle

Innkeeping Aptitude Test

As you will learn in your visits to country inns and B&Bs, success- ful innkeepers are remarkably adept at separating their personal crises from their innkeeping. Some might call it theater, others might consider it phony, but their ability to be at the door with a cheerful welcome for the arriving guest, in spite of the "calamity *du jour*," is one of the traits that set innkeepers apart from the rest of the world. It's a certain resilience of spirit not everyone possesses.

Surprisingly, most new innkeepers neglect the single most impor- tant person in their lives — themselves. Now that you have a better understanding of the industry, it is a good time to consider whether the business suits you personally. Because it's a sure bet that if you end up unhappy, no one in your entire establishment will be happy.

INNKEEPER PERSONALITY PROFILE

Do not be misled by the fact that successful innkeepers seem to have a permanently bright demeanor, endless patience, and a work ethic that would embarrass an Iowa farmer or a West Virginia coal miner. Contrary to popular myth, they weren't born that way! But they did start out with a few shared traits that are worth noting.

As you read this chapter and share some of the insights of our roundtable, look for those traits you recognize in yourself. This should give you a stronger sense of how this profession fits you. Over the next few pages, you'll see the role each of these personality "pivot points" (the "A" list) plays in the life of the successful country innkeeper.

The Innkeeper "A" List

The successful innkeeper has:

- A deep-seated love of serving other people.
- A strong entrepreneurial dedication to excellence.
- A self-effacing sense of humor.
- A stable life partnership.

The successful innkeeper is:

- A creative generalist.
- A disciplined and detail-oriented problem solver.
* A leader and motivator of staff and colleagues.
- A physically fit person dedicated to wellness.

EXPECTATIONS AND REALITY

The adult whose only knowledge of innkeeping is what he has seen of the business at that idyllic little inn in the mountains probably needs to spend some sleepless nights waiting up past midnight for the guest who never shows. Or for the plumber who finally comes two hours later than planned, at twice the hourly rate. It is vital to get a real-world sense of what goes on at the ownership level of the inn before making a career change.

Here are a few of the questions we posed to the Innkeepers' Roundtable: "How are things different for you now than you thought they might be when you entered innkeeping? What advice do you have for prospective innkeepers? What was it that finally drove you over the edge into country innkeeping? Are you glad you did it? Would you do it again?"

"When we started, we were forced into running the inn in order to generate the extra income necessary to make the mortgage pay-ment. At the start we frankly had some reservations about having strangers in our home for the night — with a key to the front door. Fortunately, our first guest, a salesman from Xerox, was so favorably impressed with our home and our hospitality he said he would not only return, but he'd tell his friends and colleagues about us as well."

The early going, for the Carters and virtually all new innkeepers, was a mammoth challenge. Like a lot of young couples, they found themselves juggling their new business and their new baby. Mark laugh-ingly reflects on the times when they were living in the house and found it necessary to load their crying baby into the car in the middle of the night to drive around town, in order to avoid disturbing their paying customers.

It is also not unusual for the fresh-faced dreamer to dramatically underestimate the personal, financial, and emotional investment the new business is going to demand.

"People often do not realize how much work there is in this business. The first year we were open, we literally worked every day without a day off — 365 of them. It was simply a matter of survival. To say that we had to hustle would be an understatement. I was used to working a lot, so the high-energy requirements of this busi-

ness were a good fit for me, but it certainly is not for everybody. It is a seven-day-a-week business for most of the people in this segment of the hospitality industry."

The Linebergers, who own the Gastonian in Savannah, were true innocents when they decided to enter the innkeeping business. They figured, quite naturally, that if they spent enough money and remodeled their inn in exacting and splendid detail, the people would beat a path to the door. Needless to say, these transplanted Californians were very disappointed when the public failed to acknowledge immediately what a splendid job they had done with the place. The good news was that for the first year and a half the Linebergers had no employee payroll overhead whatsoever. Business was so slow that they did not need to hire anyone. They were able to do all the work themselves. Fortunately, the Linebergers had sufficient financial wherewithal and intestinal fortitude to weather the early days. For them and for the Gastonian, the fun was just beginning.

"People were always telling us that we're never going to get our money out of this place, and I always responded by saying we didn't put our money into this place with one iota of thought about ever taking it back out. The Gastonian is not an investment for us — it's a love affair. And as everyone who has ever been in love can attest, the amount of money you spend is of no importance whatsoever."

Historically, the inn business is not a business to enter if making a huge annual profit is high on your list of priorities. The industry can certainly provide a comfortable, albeit challenging, lifestyle, but don't assume it can also provide a retirement nest egg. Not unlike the gambler who considers it a good day at the track when he breaks even, many innkeepers feel blessed if they can emerge at year's end with black ink of any kind on the bottom line.

As with all love affairs, the boundary between loving and loathing can be impossible to identify clearly, even in the best of times. The Innkeepers' Roundtable members from Santa Fe have experienced both, and they are still smiling!

"Innkeeping is a real 'love-hate' kind of thing. When you are up at 4:30 in the morning to serve people you might or might not know, either you like it or you don't stay in this business long. Whenever I

hit a rough spot and find myself kind of losing it, I try to busy myself with another task like selecting gift shop items. In no time it seems that I've forgotten what irritated me in the first place — all the while my husband, Pat, is busily working his usual miracles in the kitchen."

To succeed in the innkeeping business, you have to have an intuitive love for people and a deep abiding respect for serving them. If you lack either, you are destined to resent the financial and personal demands this industry will place upon you.

BEING YOURSELF

Although there are many personality traits that successful innkeepers share, part of the appeal of this industry is that they can also be themselves. Successful innkeepers are, almost without exception, mirror reflections of their typical guest, and vice versa. If you love antiques, the adventure of new places, and good food, it's a sure bet that you will attract a loyal base of repeat clients who share your interests. If you are athletically inclined and love to hike, bike, huff, and puff, you'll be a comfortable match for those inn visitors who also love an active lifestyle. You'll invariably end up creating an environment to match your own taste and style. Be careful not to create the environment you think might suit the taste of your guests . . . you might be wrong. Long after your remodeling is complete you will have to live with your creation.

Allow your operation to be a straightforward and honest extension of yourself.

"The best advice we ever got prior to getting into this business was BE YOURSELF! At first, because we were different in our approach to decor, for example, we encountered considerable subdued hostility from the owners and operators of the more traditionally decorated inns. We chose not to go the floral wallpaper route in our Victorian in order to better display the artwork on the walls, which we had managed to get on consignment from several nearby artists.

"It was a giant relief when a travel writer finally came through and praised our decision to do something different with our facility. This was an important early 'validation' experience for us. We frankly were uncertain whether we were on the right track, but we were doing our best and our property was an honest portrayal of our own taste, not to mention the constraints of our somewhat meager funds.

Fortunately, it worked! We enjoyed the open airy feeling of our home, and our guests shared our enthusiasm.

"If you like your privacy and prefer to deal with people in small doses, maybe you should avoid the inn business. If an unexpected dripping faucet or leaky roof or squirrel nest in the chimney are the kind of little irritants that make you a little crazy — for goodness sake, pick another business."

Stage of Life

Several innkeepers observed that their only regret was that they did not start into the business sooner in their lives. However, when they analyzed their feeling further they realized that they very likely would not have had the financial strength or the patience to succeed at any earlier point in their lives. The point here is that a fully developed sense of self and a stable personality are the cornerstones of successful innkeeping. This is a people-centered business that thrives on personable people serving others.

Need for Privacy

Joyce and Jim Acton entered the inn business in pursuit of their own personal lifestyle changes. Both were mature senior corporate managers with all that goes with that level of challenge. Once their youngest child had entered college, the Actons decided to leave the pressures of life in the fast lane and start a country inn. After a year of restoration they opened for guests in 1985.

The least enjoyable part of the business for Joyce Acton was the toll it exacted on her private life. As a self-described "private person," Joyce found the round-the-clock demands of operating a country inn to be extremely challenging. *"You really have no privacy when you run a country inn, especially if you actually live in the inn."*

In a similar vein, Maureen and John Magee, innkeepers at Vermont's Rabbit Hill Inn, relate that until they actually purchased a home on the property adjacent to their inn in Lower Waterford, the personal toll was enormous. As Maureen explains, *"I actually found myself in tears one evening, and it was because we lived where we worked and we simply never stopped."* Fortunately for the Magees and the loyal guests of their elegant, romantic retreat, purchasing their own quarters allowed them to maintain a healthy level of privacy just one step removed from the inn.

Joyce's advice: *"If you have a choice, consider acquiring living quarters nearby instead of living on the premises. If you live in the inn, there simply isn't a time when you're not doing business, even when you have no guests. The telephone is constantly ringing and people are incessantly at the front door, seeking a look at the inn. It can exact an enormous toll on your personal life."* That toll can manifest itself in many forms, from depression to resentment to outright hostility. Left unaddressed, those feelings invariably encroach upon the business and can ultimately lead to its demise.

It is imperative that the prospective innkeeper recognize and avoid the tendency to resent a business that takes so much time and energy. If you resent the huge sacrifices this business will require, it will show in your eyes, and you won't be successful. On the other hand, if you genuinely love serving people and do not mind subordinating your personal life to make your inn succeed, you're headed for the most exciting opportunity you've ever had.

Tolerance

How are you at accepting people who are different from you and your closest circle of friends? As an innkeeper, you will deal with every size, shape, and color of human being. If you tend to have a problem with people different from you — whether in religion, race, sexual preference, or disability — now would be a great time to reflect soberly on how you might feel about having "all of the above" over for dinner and to spend the night. If you are uncomfortable with people who are different, then this industry might not be for you.

If on the other hand, you delight in getting to know all kinds of people, you're headed into the right business, and your current peer group probably already reflects your appreciation for diversity in people. For you, the broad diversity of your guests will probably end up being the thing you love most about the business. No two days will ever be alike.

Lifestyle

Dealing with the pressures of any "people" business demands that a healthy and healthful outlook be constantly maintained. It is simply not possible to keep the schedules and meet the day-to-day challenges of life as an innkeeper without taking care of your own health. Innkeeping devours the day in such a way as to make a regular program of physical exercise almost impossible to maintain without superhuman courage and dedication. Add to that the constant exposure to wonderful aromas wafting from the kitchen at all hours of the day, an endless parade of superbly prepared dishes, high tea, and a wine tasting or two — and presto! you're ten pounds heavier. Ten pounds heavier at a time when you need to be lighter on your feet than you've ever been in your adult life.

Unless your current day-to-day routine has an innkeeper's "round the clock" regimen, you'd be well advised to begin now to adjust your own lifestyle to match the rigors of innkeeping. This means cutting down on rich foods and consuming alcohol in moderation only. You have never known temptation quite like that which will confront you daily in the kitchen of your inn. And while you're adjusting, take a hard look at how you like to spend your leisure time. There will most certainly be less of it in the days ahead, and a strict adherence to "quality" leisure time in the absence of "quantity" will be a necessity.

"We both have hobbies, but we were not able to pursue them during our seven years of innkeeping. In fact, my favorite hobby is reading, so I am almost embarrassed to admit that I did not have time to read a single book during my seven years as an innkeeper. I am sorry to say that we were not able to do very much that we just wanted to do for fun. This business is just a major drain on you personally."

Putting On a Happy Face

Part of the myth of innkeeping (and one of the reasons so many people are attracted to the business) is that all innkeepers seem to be happy all of the time. At the risk of bursting a bubble or two, let me say that's just not the case. Regardless of how poorly you feel, or what problems you are experiencing that day or that week, the reality is you've got to take a deep breath and, as one roundtable member described it, *"put on your innkeeper's face and entertain . . . it's in the job description."* Every successful innkeeper has a little bit of theatrical skill to go with their cooking, gardening, and decorating skills, and they use some of it every day of the year.

"I think it is a wonderful business, but I'm not certain it is possible to prepare anyone adequately for its challenges. I was amazed by the sheer volume of paperwork involved. But you have to get beyond the mechanics of the business and never lose sight of what is

the most important job for the innkeeper (in fact, it's one of the 'rules of the house' around here): Always remember that every guest you serve has the same kind of problems at home that we all have.

"Whether it's family, business, or money, their everyday challenges are the same as ours. When a guest visits us, he or she has chosen to spend discretionary time and money here in order to escape for a brief time from the problems of the everyday world. It is very important that we not let our problems intrude upon the pleasurable respite our guest has found here in our inn. Call it theater if you wish, but as hosts and hostesses for people at rest, we honestly believe it is the innkeeper's responsibility to ensure a pleasurable experience for our guests."

True Story

As Deedy Marble describes it, they've just concluded the fastest ten years of their lives. "At age forty-five we looked around at our universe of friends and acquaintances and were startled to realize how many of them seemed to be unhappy, and were going through some radical changes in their lives."

It was at this crossroads in their lives that Deedy and her husband Charlie decided simply to skip their mid-life crises and tackle a new career together. As a first step in that direction, the Marbles decided after twenty-five years of marriage to attend a course on values offered at the University of Massachusetts. As part of this course the instructor challenged the members of the class to write down the things they truly liked to do, and to note when they had last taken the time to do those things. "When we looked at this question we realized, like a lot of the others in our class, that we were spending most of our time doing something other than what we truly liked to do."

The Marbles began their search for a new career by analyzing how they really liked to spend their time. When they overlaid their hopes and dreams with their own skills and "held the paper up to the light," innkeeping was their next career of choice. Virtually every aspect of the business, from trying out new recipes and collecting antique knife rests to arranging flowers and teaching cooking classes, "fit" Deedy and Charlie. But even they need techniques for surviving rough spots:

"One of the most important survival hints I can convey to anyone considering getting into this wonderful crazy business is, in the interests of your own mental well-being, you must treat yourselves AT LEAST as well as you treat your guests. For us, that means beautiful scented soaps, whirlpool baths, and thick fluffy towels. If you don't occasionally turn down your own bedding, and place the rose or chocolate on your own pillow, it's just a matter of time before you grow to resent your guests and the first-class treatment they receive in your inn. Pamper each other as well as you pamper your guests . . . it's one of the most important 'perks' in our industry."

INNKEEPING AND
YOUR SIGNIFICANT OTHER

"The smartest investment I have made in this business was marrying my wife. We have grown in small increments as a team, and that strategy has worked well."

If familiarity really does breed contempt, it's a miracle that there are any lifelong partnerships out there that have been able to withstand the rigors of this profession. Like any other business partnership, personal relationships are often strained to their limits by the constant contact and shared stress of running a business. In order to take full advantage of the differences both partners bring into the enterprise, and to help preserve some degree of sanity in the relationship, it is imperative that the day-to-day duties of running the business be divided between the partners.

Additionally, each partner should understand and agree that the other will manage his or her own aspect of the business — without constant interference. This division or delineation of duties also helps ensure that the owner's imprint remains on all operating aspects of the business — thereby making it considerably less likely for important items to "slip through the cracks."

First and foremost, clarify each partner's responsibilities and duties in writing as part of a formal job description. Even though the roles and duties will inevitably overlap somewhat over time, these written job descriptions will always be there as your guide. If you launch your inn business without delineating specific areas of responsibilities, you are in essence saying you both will work on everything. That's simply not realistic. Carefully consider your respective strong suits and endeavor wherever possible to devote your energies to working in the areas of the business that match them.

Private Time

"I think the best advice I could give a prospective innkeeping couple is to make sure at least a day a week is set aside for private time together. We were terrible at disciplining ourselves to protect our private time."

Personal intimacy is often one of the first victims of an innkeeper's hectic lifestyle. Making time for each other, including time for a regular "date," will enable you both to withstand the rigors with a much healthier state of emotional well-being. You are in this together, for the long haul, and you'll be happier if you handle your lives accordingly.

"I have a difficult time even thinking about myself — much less my husband — with that 'to-do' list constantly at my elbow."

"Our favorite thing to do whenever we have a break? TAKE A NAP!"

Planning private time and space can be trickier than it sounds. It does not just happen, as you quickly learn in conversation with innkeeping couples: this idea takes some creative advance planning. This means arranging for someone else to answer the telephone and the door, and working as hard on preserving the private time as you do on taking care of the inn the remainder of the week.

"I also strongly suggest that you make time and space available for individual private time for each other. I cannot overemphasize how important this is."

Togetherness

"This business takes a lot of your time and a lot of your privacy, and it's not a business for those whose primary interest is in making money. It is a 'lifestyle change' type of business which, for better or worse, will result in your spending more time in the presence of your spouse than you could ever imagine."

If two professionals with hectic, high-powered corporate jobs requiring regular time apart decide to settle down and become innkeepers, the transition will be much more challenging than it would be for the couple who have managed their own florist business together for twelve years. If you are planning to enter the business with a partner, make it your business to explore some of the creative and very effective ways others have dealt with the personal challenges of the business.

"This is something Pat and I created together. It is definitely 'us.' Every part of our personality comes out through our inn. Both of us have grown a lot inside because of the things we've had to deal with in the inn. Because we've had to learn to deal with the staff and set policies, we've learned a lot along the way. It's made us better people. The challenging part of this business is that you have every kind of job you could ever aspire to in life, from maintenance person to PR director, from gift shop operator to chef. Each of these jobs provides a world of additional spinoff opportunities like the Christmas Bazaar we do for charity every year."

"I think this business would be difficult for a couple whose marriage or partnership is in constant need of TLC. Because of the demands of the business, if the partnership is not a strong one going in, it may very well be taxed beyond the limits of survival. People who have a fair amount of independence within their marriage are probably better suited to the inn business than those who do not. The inn business is a demanding one. Sometimes it is difficult for one or the other of the partners to realize that when the other person is busy at their 'job' it should not be construed as neglecting the marriage."

Throughout this cross-section of comments from present and former innkeepers, you are reading some of the most poignant and open remarks about the "downside" challenges of this profession that have ever appeared in print. They have been included here without hesitation because they provide an important "reality check" for those of you preparing to open and successfully operate a country inn.

"Maintaining a happy marriage is difficult enough without being co-innkeepers. When you decide to spend all day every day together eating, breathing, and sleeping innkeeping, you must be ready to accept the fact that added pressures will be placed on both parties."

"In some cases, the closeness of the business has destroyed friendships and marriages before our very eyes. In our case, these past few years have brought us much closer together."

Having the skill to operate a country inn successfully does you no good if you're not also blessed with a live-wire personality and the high energy level to match. In our conversations with innkeepers all over America, we never met one who was not a morning person. In this industry, you've either got to be a person who can hit the floor at 5:30 in the morning ready to roll — or be married to someone who is!

According to several industry observers, success in this business has less to do with money than with this propensity for hyperactivity. You've got to love staying on the go without collapsing into an exhausted heap at 2:00 in the afternoon — just as your next guests begin to arrive. The people who succeed in this business have become masters at avoiding burnout and maintaining a relentless pace of good service. They've also been able to sit down, analyze their lifestyle needs honestly, and set priorities in such a way that both business and personal life can prosper.

BURNOUT

"What I liked least about the inn business was that it was so totally consuming. It left little time for such critical and basic areas as nurturing our marriage. I must say that if a couple lacks a strong foundation in their relationship, it is easy to see how buying and operating an inn could destroy it. Our business also made it difficult or impossible to participate in the day-to-day family activities of visiting children, grandchildren, or old friends, or to attend anniversaries or birthday parties. It was just extremely difficult to get away from the inn. It is also a real challenge to take proper care of one's own personal well-being because of the day-to-day intensity of running the inn."

One innkeeper joked that if you looked up the word "burnout" in the dictionary, it would say, "*See innkeeping.*" Burnout is most often associated with "high-contact" professions. Teachers, social workers, middle-level bureaucratic functionaries, and innkeepers — all of whom must deal with the public all day, every day, on virtually the same topic — these individuals are all highly susceptible to burning out early in their careers.

Often, burnout can occur when a bright and dedicated person seems to be managed by his or her position, rather than the other way around. Whenever there is a feeling of powerlessness to alter the day-to-day tedium or course of events, burnout is close behind.

Sometimes the decision is made to enter innkeeping because of a strong need to get out of a job or a situation over which the person has little control. An overly demanding boss, a killer travel requirement, and a work situation that takes more than it gives each day can all contribute to the need to "escape" to innkeeping.   Unfortunately, the person may quickly find that he or she has escaped from a *"minimum-security honor farm to a maximum-security cell!"*

Those seeking to escape from a demanding work environment to the placid contentment of innkeeping are in for a very rude awakening. Few if any segments of the hospitality industry are as demanding and unrelenting as innkeeping. As you will see in the comments of the roundtable members throughout this section, some have handled the personal challenges of innkeeping in delightfully creative ways; others have not. Since a large proportion of those who enter the innkeeping business do so with their husband, wife, or best friend, the effects of burnout are not limited to strictly one person.

Since most inns are owner-operated affairs, you will find yourself involved in the business even when you are out of town on vacation. Constant attention to "checking on the business" makes it impossible to get away from it all. According to Jim Acton, former co-innkeeper of the White Oak Inn, *"We pretty much had to be at the inn all the time, so family and personal considerations were always secondary for us. It affected us in a lot of ways."*

Jim and Joyce Acton's contribution to the Innkeepers' Roundtable might be the most important comments of all for prospective innkeepers. By every measurable standard the Actons were a success as country innkeepers. They had a vision of a country inn in a part of the country they loved. They found the perfect little old structure, remodeled it, and began operation from ground zero. In a few years they were able to sell their successful inn business and to reap some of the financial rewards of their tireless efforts.

But in retrospect the Actons clearly consider innkeeping as a bitter-sweet experience in their lives — and not one they wish to repeat. It is hard not to be struck by the melancholy with which both of them view their time in the business. The constant demands of operating the inn took time away from the important personal side of everyday life and exacted a heavy toll on both partners. Family matters often had to remain subordinate to the needs of the business.

The signs of innkeeper burnout were clear throughout the Actons' comments. When asked what they did with their spare time, Joyce frankly admits, "We slept." Constant chronic fatigue was an everpresent reality. Inevitably, there was a sense of having lost control over one's personal agenda. Joyce lamented that she had no time to pursue her favorite pastime, reading.

Although it is difficult to second-guess financial decisions, what might the Actons have done differently?

- By broadening their geographical search beyond the central Ohio area, they might have increased the possibility of finding an existing inn for sale, which would have saved them from the costly start-up.
- More research into the primary drawing area for the White Oak Inn might have allowed them to develop a more reliable set of financial expectations.
- By offering dinner from the outset, they might have made the inn profitable sooner.
- The addition of a reliable assistant innkeeper earlier in the business might have let the Actons take greater control over their personal agenda.

Note: It takes a lot of courage to share the personal side of the innkeeping experience, especially when the story does not have a happy ending. From this author's point of view, an hour consulting with a pair of bright, intuitive, former innkeepers like Joyce and Jim Acton would be time and money well spent for any serious student of country innkeeping.

Taking Care of Yourself

A healthy lifestyle, some form of regular physical exercise, and moderation in all things are three "must dos" for those interested in a long and happy life as an innkeeper. If you have a tendency to overindulge in times of stress, you might seriously reconsider your plans to enter this profession. The day-to-day pressures of the business will inevitably exacerbate your personal problems. You're being less than honest with yourself and your partner if you fail to address those issues openly and thoughtfully before you make the deal. Plenty of issues will arise as surprises, so the more of your lifestyle habits and idiosyncrasies you can evaluate in advance the better.

Deedy and Charlie Marble have discovered the importance of rewarding themselves and making time for each other as they go about the process of running the inn. *"When my husband suffered a heart attack several years ago, we made up our minds that we would MAKE ourselves take time away from the inn on a regularly scheduled basis. These little mini-vacations have been great for our health and our own sense of well-being. These holidays are terrific times of renewal for us and we invariably return to the inn refreshed and better equipped to handle the rigors of our 14- to 16-hour days."*

The decision to take time away from the inn also forced the Marbles to begin training two assistant innkeepers they trusted. When the Marbles are not innkeeping these days they're watching films, antiquing, or off on a travel adventure.

Signs of Impending Burnout

To help you identify your own potential for innkeeper burnout, here is a list of symptoms that should not be ignored.

- Difficulty sleeping
- Increasing impatience with life's little irritations
- Less attention to your own personal well-being
- Increased consumption of drugs — including alcohol
- Increased volatility in personal relationships
- Inability to read for pleasure
- Dramatic changes in eating habits
- Unexplained weight loss or gain
- Poor concentration
- Obsessive need to "do it all"
- Mood swings
- Inability to relax
- Neglect of real vacations for yourself and your family
- Significant change in your perspective on life
- Increased depression
- A general feeling of hopelessness
- Increased cynicism
- Chronic fatigue

The closer you get to the business, the more this list will reflect the impact the wonderful world of innkeeping has had on your own life. A better understanding of the symptoms of burnout can go a long way toward helping you avoid it.

Ways to Avoid Burnout

Not everyone who enters the profession succumbs to burnout. Here are a few tips on how you can avoid burnout — in innkeeping and in life. Most important, make it your business to learn all you can about innkeeping before you enter the profession. The more you know, the more prepared you will be to avoid burnout.

Second, be realistic. Do not set yourself up for failure by obsessively attempting to make each guest's visit a perfect one. For reasons far outside your own control, some guests will enjoy your inn more than others.

Your Personal Accommodations

Many people go into the inn business with a well-thought-out plan for borrowing capital, remodeling, and devising menus but completely neglect where they themselves are going to sleep. First of all, it is imperative that you not neglect your and your partner's own comfort. If you plan to live at the inn, set the ground rules up now. This means:

- Identify your own space with a discreet plaque that makes it clear the area behind the door is private.
- Provide your guests with a telephone number that may be called in the event of an emergency. Generally, that telephone roster list begins with your manager, and includes the local emergency numbers and your private line.
- Do not attempt to live in your own guest rooms on a "space available" basis — unless you have absolutely no other choice.

Planning Private Time Away — Alone and Together

Highly motivated, driven people generally have a very difficult time preplanning a vacation — even a little one. In the inn business, the only way to survive the rigors of eighteen-hour days is to decide NOW when the inn is going to be closed for vacation or when you can be absent and entrust the inn to your staff. In addition, on a daily basis, it is important for you and your partner to support each other during the rest periods that best suit your own temperament and schedule.

Moderation in All Things

Because you are in the "entertainment" business — that is, the business of entertaining your guests — the temptation to overindulge in rich foods and alcoholic beverages can be enormous. By acknowledging those temptations, you are better equipped to deal with them effectively.

Establish a Food and Exercise Regimen

A regular schedule of physical exercise and balanced meals can be a great stabilizer for the busy innkeeper — but it is difficult to maintain. If getting out of the inn for a brisk walk or jog is difficult, then perhaps a stationary bike or treadmill might be a good idea. Since tasting foods and munching between meals are a constant in the inn business, it is important to make yourself eat nutritionally balanced meals on a regular basis. Often this means adjusting your own meal times to somewhat unusual early or late hours to accommodate your guests.

Never Stop Learning

The roundtable "pros" reached virtual unanimity on another item, the need to take — or make — the time to attend a seminar on the industry such the ones offered for prospective innkeepers by Bill Oates and Bob Fuehr.

Ways to Cut Down on Your Own Work

Plan amenities for your guests that can add to their visit without consuming your own already crowded agenda. Naturally you want to pamper your guest. The trick is figuring out how you can provide such services as restaurant recommendations, cold beverages, cookies, background on the inn, etc., without hovering over him or her.

- A collection of menus from local restaurants — complete with the comments of past guests, hours of operation, appropriate attire, etc., — kept in a family album in the common area of the inn, is an excellent way to help the guest better enjoy the area without having to personally ask for your recommendation.
- An inexpensive "office size" serve-yourself refrigerator that is accessible to your guests around the clock and kept generously stocked with soft drinks and juices is a greatly appreciated amenity.
- A "bottomless" self-service cookie jar with a lid for freshness is another great way to pamper your guests in your absence.
- Have a family album in clear view that tells the story of the creation of the inn, complete with before and after shots of your work in progress.

One very successful New England innkeeper and his wife realized early in their career that they truly enjoyed the opportunity to meet their guests prior to dinner each evening. As a result, they have a wine tasting each afternoon, and one or both of the innkeepers is always present. It would be unrealistic to make that kind of time commitment on a daily basis if they were not judicious about how they spend the other hours in their day.

REWARDS OF THE LIFESTYLE

"In spite of the hours, the business is exciting and new for us every day. We now have thirty employees and the wide diversity of management challenges we address each day makes life very interesting. It's been a very rewarding business for us. We hope our children will love this industry as much as we have."

Arguably the single greatest benefit of life as a country innkeeper is the ability to control your own destiny while doing something you love. As innkeepers, you and your partner are 100 percent in control of every aspect of the business.

There is a wide array of other advantages to the lifestyle, including:

- The people you'll meet. Few other businesses offer the opportunity to meet such a diverse group of people.
- Control of your own work schedule. That doesn't mean you'll work a leisurely eight-hour day. Few professions, in fact, demand more time every day than this one. But you can control when your inn is open for business. This means that if you decide Vermont's mud season is just no fun, and you'd rather be in the South of France . . . so be it.
- The chance to play a significant role in your community's business affairs.
- A physical plant that is an appreciating asset with each passing day.
- The ability to make a positive and lifelong impact on the lives of the people you hire and train as employees.
- The opportunity to join a select group of like-minded professionals with whom you can share and grow.

More than one innkeeper remarked how much of a pleasant surprise the lifestyle had been for their own children. A former actor and his wife, turned Nova Scotia country innkeepers, thought deeply about the impact innkeeping might have on their children. *"We can't afford to send our children around the world to experience other cultures and nationalities first-hand — but we have created the next best thing right here in our own living room!"*

During their first five years of receiving guests, they welcomed visitors from sixteen different countries — and their children managed to learn something new from each of them. These children have been shaking hands with people from all over the world since they were first able to walk. In that sense, innkeeping has been an incredible learning experience for them. *"It's as though the children have been traveling all their lives, except they've stayed in one place, right here at the inn."*

Within each country inn you visit you'll find colorful and dedicated hosts and hostesses with diverse interests incorporated into their lives as innkeepers. The unique ability to combine vocation and avocation is a genuine hallmark of the profession. For example, one innkeeper said, *"Our goal is to have one of the best kitchen gardens on the West Coast, so we spend a lot of time in our gardens. When we're not in them, we're often reading about some new aspect of gardening for the kitchen."*

Innkeepers subscribe to a variety of "lifestyle" magazines on a regular basis. Regular magazine subscriptions for the Marbles, for example, include *Gourmet, Food & Wine, Bon Appetit, Prevention, Bottom Line, Innkeeping* (the publication of the Professional Association of Innkeepers International), *Tidings* (the Independent Innkeepers Association publication), *Restaurant Hospitality, Restaurant Business, Country Life, Yankee,* and *People.*

Cooking and gardening books dominate the libraries of most country inns. *"When we're not in the inn, we like to visit other properties, food and wine festivals, and meet some of our colleagues from different parts of the country."*

True Story

The more innkeepers you encounter, the more intrigued you will become with the variety of circumstances that encourage people to enter the business in the first place. For example, the Gastonian is, in essence, Hugh and Roberta Lineberger's retirement program — except that they get very little time to rest. And the nest egg that would have gone into a comfortable retirement for this spirited couple went instead into the restoration of one of Savannah's most elegant inns.

The Linebergers are on their seventh year now and already starting on the refurbishing and replacement activity that comes with operating a high-volume facility. At present, the Gastonian is the only inn in the entire state of Georgia — and one of only a few in the entire nation — to be honored with both a AAA 4 Diamond and a Mobil 4 Star award. As Hugh proudly exclaims, "We must be doing something right!"

True Story

Only one member of the Innkeepers' Roundtable actually grew up in the inn business. Living in and around the highly acclaimed Camelback Inn, developed by her father, enabled Louise Stewart to bring a lifetime of learning to her profession as a country innkeeper. "We've found this to be a full-time 24-hour-a-day lifestyle. Since we work most holidays, we've developed an extended family of staff members and guests over the years. It's a lifestyle that suits our mentality. We now feel very attached to our lives as innkeepers. We work with people who are at rest when they are visiting so in a lot of ways we get to know them at their happiest times."

Like a lot of innkeeping partnerships, Louise and her husband, Pat, have complementary roles. Pat loves food and the creative challenge of running one of Santa Fe's most exciting and successful kitchens. Louise likes to deal with the "front of the house" side of the business.

Pat describes himself and the profession he and his family have made their life work: "I'm an old-fashioned kind of guy who loves old-style service. I love going to Europe where service is treated as an honorable profession. The inn business epitomizes that. I like serving people professionally and well, and making them happy. I just get a kick out of making other people's experience a great one."

But the business can be very challenging for family members. Louise recalls one Christmas day in particular. At 7:00 P.M. after a long day, Bumpy, their young daughter, was vacuuming the parlor after the guests' Christmas party — and the family hadn't even been home to open their own presents.

Now when Pat, Louise, and Bumpy are not innkeeping they try to act like a family and even occasionally sleep in until the scandalously late hour of 7:00 A.M. "We love to ski in season, and we try to spend our evenings at home with the family." The success of their inn has enabled them to build their dream home on the outskirts of Santa Fe, which Pat describes as "very much a work in progress."

Louise concludes: "On balance, we are proudest of the fact that we did this together. We are involved in every aspect of this business and we take great pleasure in watching it grow and prosper. This inn is our second child."

INNKEEPING APTITUDE TEST
— THE MOMENT OF TRUTH

Perhaps the single most important goal of this book is to force the aspiring innkeeper into a sober self-analysis of him or herself. To assist you in that process here is a fun and instructive exercise to help you objectively analyze how well suited you are for life as a country inn-keeper. Take the time to try this — it will be worth the trouble.

First, take a clean piece of paper and draw a "pyramid" in the following fashion: seven squares across the bottom, five in the next row above, three above that, and one on the top. Now write labels under the bottom seven boxes, *from left to right*, as follows:

Most unlike me
Unlike me
Somewhat unlike me
Undecided
Somewhat like me
Like me
Most like me

When you're done, your box should look like this diagram. Try to make it large enough so that you can place small cards or sticky notes on each square:

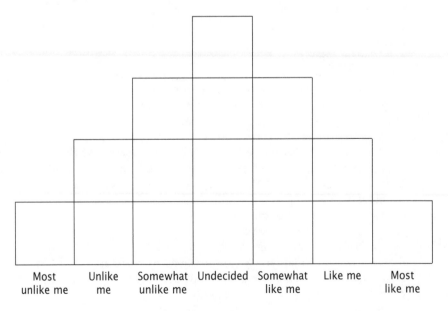

| Most unlike me | Unlike me | Somewhat unlike me | Undecided | Somewhat like me | Like me | Most like me |

Now you and your partner — this game is best played in pairs — should each take seventeen small cards or sticky notes and write on them the behaviors listed below, one for each card or note. These behaviors all play a role in the life of a country innkeeper:

> I'm a workaholic who thrives on long hours.
> I like the challenge of an unstructured work day.
> I'm an entrepreneur.
> I'm a risk taker.
> I love meeting new people.
> I like my privacy.
> I'm an optimist.
> I love serving other people
> I love to decorate.
> I love to cook.
> I handle pressure well.
> I'm a flexible person.
> I have boundless energy.
> I have a good sense of humor.
> I'm an early riser.
> I'm persistent.
> I'm creative.

Each player distributes his or her cards among the sixteen available squares, with one left over. Ideally, each of you should distribute two sets of cards — one reflecting your own feelings about each behavior and another for what you perceive to be your partner's feelings about each behavior.

After distributing the cards, discuss the results between you, weighing them and their implications for your life as an innkeeper. The discussion can be beneficial to you in several ways.

First, compare your sort of your own behaviors to your partner's sort of his or her own behaviors. Generally, the greater the differences between the two — the more different you are from each other — the stronger and more successful the innkeeper partnership will be. If you find you prefer more of a "back of the house" role while your partner is the ebullient "people-greeter" type, so be it. In this business, you'll find there are plenty of jobs to go around.

Second, pay particularly close attention to the behavior "left over" after all the others have been positioned on the board. The one left over is, by definition, the one you're least "decided" about — or, to put it another way, most ambivalent about. The more fundamental this left-over behavior is to success as an innkeeper, the more seriously you should give second thoughts to becoming an innkeeper. For example, if "I love meeting new people" is your left-over behavior, you might well conclude that innkeeping is not really for you.

On the other hand, if "I love to decorate" — also a positive trait for an innkeeper — is the one remaining, it might not be the end of the world. It may be that your partner feels more strongly and positively about this particular behavior, and can assume this particular chore. Alternatively, decorating is one behavior that, if both of you are indifferent to it, can be purchased.

Finally, look now at the difference between the sort of your own behavioral priorities and your partner's sort of your behaviors . . . as he or she perceives you. The differences can reveal quite a lot about how candid you are with yourself and with others. If you believe you love to meet people, but your partner is not so sure that's your strong point, what does that mean for your life as an innkeeper?

After all this comparing and contrasting, you should have reached some revealing conclusions about yourself. Are you still persuaded that you both have, between you, the requisite preferences for innkeeping behaviors that will help you succeed?

If so, great! You've passed an important first lesson on becoming an innkeeper. And if you can tackle the risk of a new business with an open mind, maintaining your sense of humor and your enthusiasm (as you've doubtless been forced to do during this little behavioral game), then you're a good candidate for this industry. Bring your good attitude and sense of humor along. You're going to need them, as you take the next step toward opening and successfully operating a country inn.

Part Two

OPENING YOUR COUNTRY INN

The Queen Victoria Bed & Breakfast, Cape May, New Jersey.

VINCE MARCHESE

Chapter Four

THE BUSINESS OF INNKEEPING

Starting the Business

Structuring the Business
The Sole Proprietorship
The Partnership
The Corporation

STARTING THE BUSINESS

Opening and operating a successful country inn begins with you recognizing first and foremost that your inn is, in fact, your business. You would never launch any new business venture without the support and good counsel of a team of experts, and that includes innkeeping. Because you and your immediate partners bring skills of your own to the enterprise, the varied strengths of the outsiders you bring into your group will be determined by where you need help the most. For example, if your background is real estate, marketing, or law, you can generally provide your operation with management expertise in those disciplines and retain outside counsel only in those areas where you and your partner perhaps are not as strong. Generally, your team of professionals will include:

A real estate broker who understands the real estate market and the local regulations pertaining to fair market values and transfer of property. *Note:* This broker should not be the same person who is representing the seller of the property you are planning to acquire. You want your agent to be concentrating on only one person's best interests . . . YOURS.

An attorney licensed to practice in the state where you plan to do business. Here once again, it is preferable that you locate counsel with some background on the market you are entering, particularly if you have no prior experience in that market yourself. In addition, your lawyer should be thoroughly experienced in new business start-ups, and the closer his or her background to the lodging, food, and beverage industry, the better! Take advantage of the advice and counsel of other innkeepers. The greatest trial lawyer in America is probably not the best-suited attorney to assist you in acquiring a country inn.

An accountant with direct and relevant prior experience in the inn business will save you a lot of money in the long run. This accountant need not necessarily be one of the "Big Eight" (and big buck) firms; in fact, the bulk of your financial report preparation and end of the year tax filing can probably be handled quite effectively by a bookkeeper. But don't skimp on a tight and accurate system of operations procedures and reporting from Day One. It is not unusual for an entrepreneur to take a very casual approach to the accounting and record-keeping side of a new business. It is important to realize that the time to set up your record-keeping system is before, not after, you start your business. Later on, when it comes time to expand or sell the inn, you will be justifiably rewarded for your attention to detail in the early days of the business.

A banker, preferably one you have worked with for a reasonable period of time. Whether you plan to fund your start-up through debt (borrowed) or equity (your own) financing, your banker can be a genuine asset in helping you understand the current interest rates, available credit terms, and qualification requirements. If your banker is not the source you will tap for initial capital, he or she may very well be in a position to suggest some alternatives based on the local business climate.

An insurance agent might not sound like a critically important addition to your team of human resources and advisors, but he or she certainly is. Insuring your business is quite different from securing automobile or homeowner's insurance. Competent professional assistance in securing the necessary insurance to fully protect your new business should be high on your list of start-up priorities.

A building contractor who is familiar with renovations will be a particularly important addition to the team if you are planning to acquire an existing structure. If the structure has not been previously operated as an inn, your contractor will be a big help in getting a clear and concise idea of the costs of bringing the property up to your operating requirements, and even more importantly, up to compliance with the local codes and ordinances.

An inn consultant would not have been a consideration in the "early days" (fifteen or twenty years ago) of the innkeeping business. But as the industry has grown and prospered in recent years, a number of bright competent folks have "hung out the shingle" and now provide comprehensive consultation services in every aspect of the business. Many of these consultants are former innkeepers, and you'll find their information and input quite thought provoking.

For an up-to-date list of inn consultants, as well as suppliers of inn products and services such as private label amenities, apprenticeship programs, computer software reservation systems, decorating assistance, and even professional innsitters, your best one-stop reference tool is: **Country Inns Yellow Pages, P.O. Box 1789, Kankakee, IL 60901, (815-939-3509).** The various inn associations and professional support groups outlined in the Appendix on pages 213 to 222 of this book can also provide you with a starting list of human resources which you might find valuable to starting your business.

STRUCTURING THE BUSINESS

The financial and legal members of your team will be able to provide you with guidance relative to which operating structure is best for your own personal needs. In essence, you have three basic options. You may choose to operate your country inn as a sole proprietorship, a partnership, or a corporation. Each business structure has its own unique advantages and limitations, and it is not possible to counsel you on which approach might best suit your needs without first-hand knowledge of your personal finances and long-range goals for the business. All three basic structures are very briefly outlined below.

The Sole Proprietorship

The simplest form of business structure available to you is the sole proprietorship. The sole proprietorship is essentially a business with only one owner (or one couple), which may be set up for very little money and virtually no formal approval process. You will need to acquire whatever local business licenses may be applicable in your area, but other than those, your business, as the name implies, is basically a "one man" or "one woman" show. That means you are personally liable for the obligations of the proprietorship, and you have sole claim to any profits which the business generates.

A sole proprietorship is the most informal business structure, and the most limited. Your ability to borrow money is generally limited in a sole proprietorship, and the opportunities for expansion at a later date through the sale of equity are extremely limited. Because of its simplicity, a sole proprietorship is sometimes set up initially at the start-up of an enterprise, and later converted to one of the other more flexible forms of ownership as the business matures. Sole proprietorships are more appropriate to limited income homestays and B&Bs, which can be established with very little borrowing.

The Partnership

The formal definition of a partnership is "an association of two or more persons to carry on as co-owners of a business for profit." Partnerships have two types or classes of partner: limited partners, who are essentially part of the organization because of their contribution of capital (but who might also be included for their management expertise); and general partners, who are liable for the affairs of the partnership and who may or may not also have a capital interest in the partnership.

Partnerships are somewhat more cumbersome from the standpoint of paperwork, and fall between the sole proprietorship and the corporation in terms of the ease with which long-term financing might be arranged for the business. From a practical standpoint, a partnership might make sense for a country innkeeper who is interested in bringing in a limited amount of additional capital and who has no personal concerns about the unlimited personal liability aspects of the structure.

The Corporation

The corporation is the most complex structural option available to you, and for several reasons may be your best operating alternative. A corporation is defined as "an artificial being, invisible, intangible, and existing only in contemplation of the law." Corporations must be set up in accordance with state and federal law and formally approved by the secretary of state where the corporation is domiciled. Although this might sound complicated, your legal counsel can, and often does, handle virtually every aspect of the corporation's structural compliance with the law.

Once incorporated, your personal liability is limited generally to the amount of your investment in the organization, and it is a simple matter to transfer ownership of stock, sell additional stock to raise capital, and/or pledge the assets of the corporation for the purposes of securing long-term capitalization. A frequent ownership option, particularly for new country innkeepers who contemplate several years of operating losses in the start-up phase of the inn, is the Subchapter "S" corporation which permits the losses of the corporation to be "passed through" to the shareholders, while still maintaining the liability protection of the "corporate shield." A Subchapter S corporation is a common form of business structure, and your legal and financial advisors can explain whether it suits your needs.

A lot of the discussion regarding opening your country inn presupposes you have already located either an existing inn that is a suitable candidate for acquisition or the perfectly located fine old building that might be "upfitted" for its new life as a country inn. Whichever alternative you've selected, a carefully assembled development plan for how you propose to proceed after the acquisition is your next appropriate step.

*Stained glass highlights the Swiss dining room of Chalet Suzanne,
Lake Wales, Florida.*

Chapter Five

THE BUSINESS PLAN

The Executive Summary

Property/Business Description

The Marketing Plan
>Whom do You Plan to Serve?
>How Do You Plan to Reach Your Market?

Operations and Management

Financial Projections
>Income Projections
>Expense Projections
>Cash Flow Projections
>Capital Needs
>Sources of Capital
>Financial Statement

Think of the business plan for your inn as the "keel in the water" for this great entrepreneurial adventure. Although all business plans contain essentially the same fundamental elements — executive profile, business description, marketing plan, operations plan, and financial summary — no two business plans are ever the same. Nor should they be. The business plan for your inn should read in such a way as to entice the reader into each subsequent section. A well-thought-out business plan is the framework of your business and, as such, needs to begin with a foundation.

THE EXECUTIVE SUMMARY

The Executive Summary or Executive Profile is the narrative recap you will write after you have written the entire business plan. Since it will be the first item presented in the plan, it should provide a tantalizing sampler of all the information contained in your business plan. It should be written to be read by people who have very little time to waste on ill-conceived notions — because that's exactly who will be reading it.

The summary should briefly and concisely restate:

• a basic description of the proposed business
• the goals and objectives of the business
• how you plan to incorporate your talents and the talents of your management team into a successful and profitable enterprise

It's OK to do a little "selling" with your summary page. A description of "chestnuts roasting on an open fire" might get even the crustiest loan officer's wheels turning. The summary should also contain sufficient narrative material to give the reader a feel for what will make your country inn different from all other inns, and enough broad financial information to let the reader know you are going into the business with your eyes open. In addition, the plan should convey that you understand the importance of timely and proper debt service, and that your projections are sufficiently realistic that you will be able to honor your obligations even if things don't quite go exactly as you've planned.

PROPERTY/BUSINESS DESCRIPTION

The property and business description of your country inn should include not only the legal description of the property you plan to acquire but an overview of the structure of business you have chosen, i.e., sole proprietorship, partnership, or corporation. The descriptive section of your business plan should also contain as much of a detailed description of the common areas as possible, i.e., entry hall, foyer, library, dining room. Overall descriptions of the furnishings in each guest room including accessories, style, and theme would be considered appropriate additions to the description section of your business plan, as would a brief history of the property, including why, in your opinion, it is well suited for operation as a country inn. The more detail you can provide relative to square footage in "back of the house" service areas such as kitchen and prep space, the more the reader will see that you have done your homework.

Guard against making your property description a cold hard laundry list of facts and figures. It is perfectly OK to paint a word picture of the inn as you see it in your own mind and heart after you've put your own imprint in place. Remember, if your vision for the finished product is unclear, so is everyone else's!

THE MARKETING PLAN

Your marketing plan is where you get to show off the homework you've already done on your competitive environment. The research you've completed on the current market condition, including guest room inventories, rate of occupancy, room rates, restaurant prices, and food service trends, should be supplemented by the more global market data you have secured from the chamber of commerce and the convention and visitors bureau. The research you have put into your project may very well be the most important and most revealing part of your business plan.

Research and pragmatic conservatism can be a prospective innkeeper's best friends.

"Before we made the decision to get into this business, our primary market research consisted of staying in inns in the area. We learned some things to do and some things not to do, and based strictly upon the sheer demand for rooms in this area we concluded

*this might be a great place to run an inn. We went through a very
basic cost analysis and projected our income and expenses on the
basis of a 45 percent occupancy rate. We concluded, based upon
these projections, that we broke even and began making money at
around 45 percent overall year-round occupancy. As it turned out
we were low on our estimated expenses — but fortunately, we were
also low on our projected occupancy. Our advice is carefully project
your expenses — and then add 20 or 25 percent to that projection.*

*"We have been lucky in that we've consistently operated at a 90
percent annual rate of occupancy over the past several years and
that has more than compensated for our higher-than-projected expenses. When I speak with our innkeeper friends in other areas, it is
clear that our higher occupancy figures carry with them considerably
higher costs of doing business. For example, we have to have a full-
time staff person just to answer the telephone for our inn."*

Whom Do You Plan To Serve?

Your marketing plan should next address your target customer. A
precise description of your primary, secondary, and tertiary markets,
who they are, where they are, and how you propose to reach them, are
all equally important components of the plan. The better you understand who your market is, the easier it will be to convince others that
not only have you carefully analyzed the marketplace but that a target
does actually exist. By further embellishing your target market identifi-
cation with secondary and tertiary targets, you communicate your understanding that there must always be a plan "B," and that you are
prepared to exploit it as needed.

Make certain you include in your marketing plan any ancillary selling opportunities you plan to incorporate into your business. Souvenir
personalized amenities, cookbooks, candles, stuffed rabbits, and T-shirts
have become a vital revenue generator in the country inn segment and
should not be overlooked in the overall marketing plan. If you plan to
incorporate a cooking school, flower arranging, or any other signature
products or services into your overall package, those plans should be
included as well.

How Do You Plan to Reach Your Market?

Now that you've researched the market sufficiently to know that an
opportunity for a country inn exists, and examined the marketplace

closely enough to identify who might buy the goods and services your inn will offer, it's time to address exactly how you will reach your target customer. You have already identified those public relations and marketing opportunities that exist for your new business. Now it is simply a matter of sorting out what communications alternatives are available, how you can most effectively exploit each, and how much you are going to spend to accomplish your occupancy goals.

For example, let's assume your first order of business is the creation and production of your inn's logo, followed immediately by your brochure, business card, letterhead, and envelopes. Explain in your business plan when you plan to produce these materials, how much money you have budgeted for their production, and how you plan to integrate each into your marketing communications program. If you plan to hold an open house for the garden club, or a press party for the local media to get a look at your facility, include a brief statement of the specifics in your plan.

OPERATIONS AND MANAGEMENT

This section of your business plan is your opportunity to show the reader that you have a grasp of the real world of innkeeping, even if you are grasping with a sweaty palm at this point. In the operations and management section of your business plan, it is appropriate to outline the chosen business structure and to explain why it is best suited to your needs. Identify all key management personnel and provide one-page resumes on each. Although some business advisors disagree on how much biographical information might be appropriately included at this stage of the business plan, it's a good idea to include more, not less, than might be needed.

Even though you and your partner are the primary employees of the business, it is a good idea to include the professional profiles of the other members of the management team, i.e., accountant, attorney, real estate, and inn consultant. The person reading the business plan will understand that these are not full-time paid employees of the business, but it will be clear that you have taken time to supplement the skills of the principals where necessary. A brief description of each "department" in your inn and the duties assigned to the person overseeing it, as well as the projected range of compensation, helps round out the reader's understanding of how you plan to run the business.

FINANCIAL PROJECTIONS

The importance of the financial section of your business plan is directly related to your need to raise funding for your venture. The more need you have for "outside" funding (for the sake of this discussion, "outside" funding is defined as monies secured outside your immediate family), the more critical the financial section of your business plan will be. The financial projection section of the business plan will contain (in their relative order of importance):

- Cash Flow, Revenue Projections
- Projected Capital Requirements/Source of Capital
- Personal Financial Statement

In addition, and depending once again on how much outside assistance you will be seeking, you might also include an analysis of the various owner benefits which will be arising from your living on the premises. When an outside investor realizes how much direct benefit the owner/operator receives, and how many direct living expenses such as housing, utilities, food, insurance, auto expenses, travel and entertainment, cleaning, consumable supplies, etc., are covered by the inn, the financier can more clearly understand the drastically reduced monthly salary requirements of the innkeeper.

In order to help you organize your own income and expense projections, and to establish a consistent standard of comparison for the country inn/bed and breakfast operators, the Professional Association of Independent Innkeepers International has developed the following sample chart of accounts.

Country Inn Chart of Accounts

REVENUE ACCOUNTS

Room Revenue
Food Revenue
Beverage Revenue
Gift Shop Revenue
Specialty Food Service Revenue
Cooking Classes/Other Revenue

OPERATING EXPENSE ACCOUNTS	S.P.O.E.*
Food & Beverage (hourly or part-time)	4.5
Food & Beverage (salaried)	
Room Related (hourly or part-time)	7.5
Room Related (salaried)	
Auto	2
Bank Fees	
Business Taxes & Fees	3.5
Commissions	
Dues & Subscriptions	1
Food	9
Insurance	5
Interest	30
Legal & Accounting Fees	1
Maintenance, Repairs & Fixtures	4
Marketing — Advertising & Promotion	8
Miscellaneous	
Office Supplies & Postage	1
Outside Services	4
Owner Wages or Draw	
Postage	1
Professional Education	
Room & Housekeeping Supplies	4
Salaried or Permanent Employees	5
Telephone	2
Towels & Linens	1.5
Training	
Travel & Entertainment	
Utilities	6

* Standard Percentage of Expenses.

The preceding *Innkeeper Chart of Accounts* is reprinted by permission of the Professional Association of Innkeepers International, P.O. Box 90710, Santa Barbara, CA 93190 (805-569-1853).

Your own Chart of Accounts might of course vary slightly from this one. If, for example, you plan to offer horseback riding as a revenue generator, it should be added to the revenue account section. The following Chart of Accounts, provided as an additional example by one of the roundtable members, includes asset and liability accounts as well as income and expense accounts.

Chart of Accounts

Account Number	Type	Name
1010	Cash	Checking Account
1013	Cash	Cash on Hand
1017	Current Asset	Savings Account
1020	Current Asset	Prepaid Interest
1030	Current Asset	Prepaid Insurance
1040	Current Asset	Prepaid Taxes
1059	Current Asset	Accounts Receivable
1059/0001	Current Asset	A/R — Credit Cards
1059/1002	Current Asset	A/R House — Lodging
1059/1003	Current Asset	A/R House — Restaurant
1500	Inventory	Inventory
1500/20	Inventory	Inventory — Food
1500/30	Inventory	Inventory — Food
1500/40	Inventory	Inventory — Miscellaneous
1505	Inventory	Purchases
1505/20	Inventory	Purchases — Food
1505/30	Inventory	Purchases — Beverage
1700	Fixed Asset	Buildings
1701	Fixed Asset	Accum. Deprn. — Buildings
1705	Fixed Asset	Restaurant Furniture and Fixtures
1706	Fixed Asset	Accum. Deprn. — Rest. Furn. and Fixtures
1708	Fixed Asset	Furniture and Fixtures
1709	Fixed Asset	Accum. Deprn. — Furniture and Fixtures
1710	Fixed Asset	Vehicles
1711	Fixed Asset	Accum. Deprn. — Vehicles
1712	Fixed Asset	Equipment
1713	Fixed Asset	Accum. Deprn. — Equipment
1714	Fixed Asset	Land
1715	Fixed Asset	Land Improvements
1716	Fixed Asset	Accum. Deprn. — Land Improvements
1717	Other Asset	Good Will
1720	Other Asset	Organization Expenses
1721	Other Asset	Accum. Amort. — Organization Expenses
2000	Current Liability	Accrued General Expenses
2002	Current Liability	Accrued Rooms and Meals Tax
2004	Current Liability	Accrued Real Estate Taxes
2018	Current Liability	Total Payroll Taxes Payable
2018/0001	Current Liability	Federal
2018/0002	Current Liability	FICA

2018/0003	Current Liability	State
2018/0004	Current Liability	FUTA
2018/0005	Current Liability	State Unemployment Tax
2018/0006	Current Liability	Medicare Tax
2020	Current Liability	Insurance Payable
2059	Current Liability	Accounts Payable — Guests
2059/0001	Current Liability	A/P — Trade
2059/0002	Current Liability	A/P — Guests
2060	Current Liability	Gratuities
2070	Current Liability	Gift Certificates
2100	Current Liability	Advance Deposits
2100/0001	Current Liability	Advance Deposits — Lodging
2100/0002	Current Liability	Advance Deposits — Restaurants
2505	Long-Term Liability	Loan — Commercial Bank
2507	Long-Term Liability	Credit Line — Commercial Bank
2510	Long-Term Liability	Loan — Owners
3000	Equity	Capital Stock
3010	Equity	Retained Earnings (Loss)
3100	Close	Retained Earnings
4010/10	Revenue	Lodging
4020	Revenue	Food
4030/30	Revenue	Beverage
4040/40	Revenue	Miscellaneous
4050	Revenue	Interest
5010	Cost of Goods Sold	Cost of Goods Sold
5010/10	Cost of Goods Sold	Cost of Goods Sold — Lodging
5010/20	Cost of Goods Sold	Cost of Goods Sold — Food
5010/30	Cost of Goods Sold	Cost of Goods Sold — Beverage
5010/40	Cost of Goods Sold	Cost of Goods Sold — Miscellaneous
6000	Expense	Wages — Officers
6001	Expense	Wages — Other
6001/10	Expense	Wages — Lodging
6001/20	Expense	Wages — Food
6001/30	Expense	Wages — Beverage
6003	Expense	Payroll Taxes
6003/0002	Expense	FICA
6003/0004	Expense	FUTA
6003/0005	Expense	State Unemployment Tax
6003/0006	Expense	Medicare Tax
6010	Expense	Advertising
6015	Expense	Bank Charges
6017	Expense	Commissions — Credit Card

6017/0001	Expense	Visa/MC
6017/0002	Expense	American Express
6019	Expense	Commissions — Travel Agents
6020	Expense	Donations
6021	Expense	Dues and Subscriptions
6022	Expense	Gas and Oil
6023	Expense	Grounds
6024	Expense	Guest Entertainment
6025	Expense	Insurance
6030	Expense	Interest
6032	Expense	Laundry and Linen
6033	Expense	License and Fees
6034	Expense	Vending Supplies
6036/30	Expense	Bar Supplies
6037	Expense	Kitchen Supplies
6038	Expense	Dining Room Supplies
6039	Expense	Room Supplies
6040	Expense	Postage
6053	Expense	Office Supplies
6056	Expense	Printing
6057	Expense	Professional Services
6057/0001	Expense	Legal Fees
6057/0002	Expense	Accounting Fees
6058	Expense	Repairs and Maintenance
6059	Expense	Taxes — Real Estate
6060	Expense	Taxes — Other
6061	Expense	Utilities
6061/0001	Expense	Oil
6061/0002	Expense	Gas
6061/0003	Expense	Electric
6061/0004	Expense	Cable TV
6063	Expense	Sewer
6065	Expense	Telephone
6068	Expense	Trash Removal
6070	Expense	Travel
6200	Expense	Miscellaneous
7500	Other Income/Expense	Depreciation
7500/0001	Other Income/Expense	Depreciation — Buildings
7500/0002	Other Income/Expense	Depreciation — Furniture and Fixtures
7500/0003	Other Income/Expense	Depreciation — Vehicles
7500/0004	Other Income/Expense	Depreciation — Equipment
7500/0005	Other Income/Expense	Depreciation — Restaurant Furn & Fix
7500/0006	Other Income/Expense	Depreciation — Land Improvements
7700	Other Income/Expense	Amortization

When you prepare and present your own chart of accounts as part of the financial section of your business plan, it is a good idea to extend each account heading in horizontal rows divided vertically by month. Every twelve months a separate column clearly labeled "Annual Total" would make the summary easier to read and to understand.

Income Projections

If you find projecting revenue a bewildering challenge, you are not alone. It is not possible to know with absolute certainty how many guest rooms you will rent over a given period of time, but it is possible to do some conservative projections that will begin to get you closer to the actual number than you are at this moment.

For the purposes of this example, assume the average occupancy rate for the community where you plan to operate is 56 percent. That means that for all properties that rent overnight accommodations in your area, 56 percent of the available inventory of guest rooms is rented overall. If you are planning to include dinner in your country inn package as a Modified American Plan (MAP) offering, it would be helpful to separate the projected cost of the evening meal.

A new country inn in the market should conservatively expect to operate at an occupancy rate of 50 percent of the overall market average in Year One, and depending upon the success of word of mouth, increase annual occupancy at the rate of 10 percent each year. In this example, therefore, Year One occupancy would be projected at 28 percent (1/2 of 56 percent). If your inn has twelve guest rooms available for rental seven nights each week, the weekly total is eighty-four. Assuming the inn is closed for vacation two weeks each year, and open to the public the remaining fifty weeks, the total annual available room nights at your inn is fifty times eighty-four, or 4,200 room nights. If your first-year occupancy is indeed 28 percent, the total room nights sold in Year One would be 28 percent of 4,200, or 1,176.

If your average MAP rate is $115, and you allocate $25 of that to your dinner meal, your B&B rate per night would be $90. To project the room revenues for Year One based on the 28 percent occupancy rate, simply multiply $90 times 1,176 to get $105,840.

You get the idea. The key point is BE CONSERVATIVE. If you are able to create and execute a business plan that survives at a first-year occupancy rate of 28 percent, just imagine what a pleasure it will be to run the business at a 45 or 50 percent rate!

Lenders like to see that the entrepreneur has gone the extra mile to analyze the market, above and beyond the obvious. For example, in addition to a summary on what is happening in the market relative to inns of the same basic size and a description of the proposed property, you might consider including an analysis of souvenir and gift shop sales in the area, or off-premise catering, if either business segment is relevant to your planned operation.

Expense Projections

As innkeeping has matured into a full-fledged segment of the hospitality industry, it has begun to generate more industry-wide data and specific detail on the cost of doing business in various size inns all over America. Once again, the leader in generating this data has been the Professional Association of Innkeepers International, PAII.

PAII has surveyed the recipients of its *Innkeeping* newsletter and determined the annual expenses (without innkeeper salaries, capital expenditures, or depreciation) for an inn to be approximately $11,000 per room. Note the judicious use of the word *approximately* here. PAII bases its numbers on those inns who responded to its questionnaire, and although those numbers are instructive, they represent the comparatively limited number of facilities who both subscribe to *Innkeeping* and were willing to share their operating numbers with the association.

PAII has also generated an extremely helpful "Standard Percentage of Expenses" (SPOE) based upon their survey results. Your own expense percentages will of course vary somewhat from these figures based upon the costs of doing business in your part of the country. In order to give you a sense of how actual expenses might vary from the SPOE numbers generated by PAII, the *Real Estate Appraiser and Analyst* prepared the following copy of an actual operating statement for an eighteen-room inn located in coastal California. This particular property has no restaurant, therefore no allowance for revenues and expenses arising from public meal service is considered.

Eighteen-Room Inn Annual Operating Expenses

Category	Amount	% of total	Comments
Property Taxes	$32,500	8.00	adjusted fair market value basis
Insurance	9,600	2.50	fire, liability, contents, etc.
Local Taxes and License	14,400	4.00	excludes room tax @ 8 percent
Salaries - Innkeepers	96,000	24.40	all management full-time employees
Wages - Housekeeping	37,000	9.19	hired at various hourly rates
Maintenance	18,000	4.06	includes gardening and minor repairs
Payroll Taxes & Workers' Comp.	39,100	9.95	
Employee Health Plan	7,000	2.00	
Utilities	25,000	6.04	electricity, propane gas, water only; excludes sewer: property on septic
Advertising/Promotion	30,000	7.60	includes literature and mailing costs
Office Expenses	6,600	1.70	on premises
Housekeeping Maintenance and Supplies	30,000	7.69	includes guest room maintenance and redecorating, linens, etc.
Food and Beverage	32,000	8.20	wastage and employee use +/- 10 percent
Repairs and Maintenance	12,000	3.10	general preventative maintenance
Miscellaneous	3,000	.76	
Total Operating Expenses	$393,300	100.00	
Added by Appraiser for General Reserves	19,700		based on .05 percent of expenses
Total Operating Expenses	$413,000		

The following is an actual 1993 budgeted income statement for a fifteen-room country inn in New England with a full service dining room which is open to the public:

Income Statement — Twelve Months

Operating Revenues	Budget	
Lodging	$275,000	51.8%
Food	$200,000	37.7%
Beverage	$50,000	9.4%
Miscellaneous	$6,000	1.1%
Net Operating Revenues	$531,000	100.0%
Cost of Goods Sold	$98,000	18.5%
Gross Profit	$433,000	81.5%
General and Administrative Expense		
Wages — Officers	$30,000	5.6%
Wages — Other	$110,000	20.7%
Payroll Taxes	$30,000	5.6%
Advertising	$19,000	3.6%
Commissions — Credit Card	$8,000	1.5%
Commissions — Travel Agents	$2,000	0.4%
Donations	$1,000	0.2%
Dues and Subscriptions	$3,000	0.6%
Gas and Oil	$2,500	0.5%
Grounds	$1,000	0.2%
Insurance	$19,000	3.6%
Interest	$63,000	11.9%
Laundry and Linen	$10,000	1.9%
License and Fees	$750	0.1%
Kitchen Supplies	$3,000	0.6%
Dining Room and Bar Supplies	$2,500	0.5%
Room Supplies	$5,000	0.9%
Postage	$7,000	1.3%
Office Supplies	$2,000	0.4%
Printing	$2,500	0.5%
Professional Services	$1,000	0.2%
Repairs and Maintenance	$8,000	1.5%
Taxes	$7,000	1.3%
Utilities	$19,000	3.6%
Sewer	$3,900	0.7%

Telephone	$5,000	0.9%
Trash Removal	$1,400	0.3%
Travel	$2,000	0.4%
Miscellaneous	$500	0.1%

Total General and Administrative Expense	$369,050	69.5%

Net Operating Profit	$63,950	12.0%
Depreciation & Amortization	$40,000	7.5%
Net Income	$23,950	4.5%

Cash Flow Projections

The cash flow projection for your country inn is determined by subtracting the expenses from the income. It might be a good idea to sit down first. It is not unusual for the net cash flow to be a net operating deficit in the early years of your business. In addition, in order to calculate the actual cash flow available for debt service, the interest and depreciation must be added back into the equation. In the above illustration, the net income of $23,950 would be added to $63,000 in interest and $40,000 in depreciation, for a total cash flow available for debt service of $126,950.

Your cash flow projections should be prepared by month for a minimum of three years, and by year for three more years. Clearly, the early numbers will carry considerably more weight with your financiers than the later ones, but all of your numbers should be generated in as conservative a manner as possible. Financial "types" do not like surprises — unless they are good ones. Develop a habit of approaching your financial projections with a cold hard "realistic" sharp pencil and you will quickly earn a reputation with your backers as someone whose numbers can be trusted.

One roundtable member stated flatly that no matter how conservative you are, you will always underestimate start-up costs. The furnace will break; the roof will leak; the pump will need to be replaced. The best idea is to be conservative about your expense projections — and then double them.

Once you have developed your cash flow projections, you can then generate a break-even occupancy level to serve as your target. To arrive at a break-even occupancy percentage, simply divide the lodging or room-related expenses by the total room income of the facility when fully occupied. In the new inn described in the Income Projection on page 95, there are a total of 4,200 room nights generating a total income of $378,000 at 100 percent occupancy. If the total annual expenses of the new inn are $124,000, the break-even occupancy percentage is $124,000 divided by $378,000, equaling 32.8 or 33 percent. As you can see from the example, if the new inn operates at the projected rate of 28 percent in Year One, and increases to 38 percent in Year Two, the inn should be breaking into black ink between the second and third year of operation.

Capital Needs

Servicing the negative cash flow is an important part of the projected Capital Requirement / Source of Capital Summary. How you plan to survive long enough to get to profitability and where you plan to get the funds are two vitally important issues to your prospective banker and/or partners. Through realistic summary of the capital needs and source of funds should be included in the financial section of your business plan.

Your capital needs summary should include:

- Start-up costs, such as remodeling, bath additions, decorative accessories
- Down payment
- Working capital
- Closing costs
- Miscellaneous expenses
- Negative cash flow funding

Obviously, the capital needs recap should clearly indicate sufficient financial strength to survive the early projected operating deficits for the inn.

Sources of Capital

Your primary sources for capitalizing your inn (over and above the first mortgage on the inn property itself) will be your own personal assets. Due to the intense, hands-on nature of inn ownership and management, it is highly unlikely capital can — or should — be raised from uninvolved third party investors. Your own sources of capital might include: sale of vacation condo, sale of boat, liquidation of common stock, retirement/termination settlement, profit-sharing funds from your former employer, savings account, or net from sale of primary residence.

Financial Statement

The final element of your financial section is your own personal financial statement and/or the financial statement for your own business if you have owned and operated a business which reflects your skill for generating a profit. In all likelihood any credit lines and/or outright bank loans you seek for the business will require your personal endorsement. In order to consider the strength of the endorsement, the financial institution will need as much comprehensive and current financial information as you are able to provide. Your bank or S&L will be happy to provide you with a blank financial statment that suits their needs and criteria. The extent of your preparedness for the initial round of conversations with your projected lender will reveal quite a lot about your preparedness for assuming the responsibility for opening and operating your own business.

Chapter Six

PERMITS AND INSURANCE

Zoning and Planning

Health and Safety

Public Works/Taxes/Licences

Insurance

ZONING AND PLANNING

At the local and municipal level, building and zoning ordinances vary considerably. This is one area where being overly cautious is the order of the day. Depending upon where you are, there may not even be existing ordinances to cover the operation of a country inn. If that is the case, be ready to supply your local officials with a copy of the ordinances that cover other cities in your region, or a copy of the suggested copy of the ordinances as supplied by one of the professional support groups.

Generally, what you plan to do with this venerable old structure will prove enormously beneficial to the community and the neighborhood, but be prepared to prove it with your own plans, renderings, even menus if you have them ready. Even the most difficult zoning restrictions can be managed through the granting of "variances" on an as-needed basis. Your architect and your attorney can both be extremely helpful to you throughout this process.

"Looking back on it, if we had it to do over again, I think we would have worked harder earlier in the game to inform the local officials about our industry and our business. If you are getting ready to take the plunge into the inn business you'd be well advised to make it a point to sit down with the local zoning authorities and do whatever you can to help them better understand the innkeeping industry. If you can make them an ally at the outset you'll be a lot better off. Redevelopment is a fuzzy discipline at best and taking the initiative to lead the way is often better than waiting for a vote which goes against you."

HEALTH AND SAFETY

Here once again, the rules vary widely from city to city, but essentially, the local health department (and all other municipal departments charged with licensing and inspections) should be viewed as your ally, not your opposition. The people who are charged with public health and safety have a huge responsibility and are often woefully understaffed for the task at hand. They are primarily interested in the steps you are taking to ensure water quality, appropriate disposal of all sewage, and cleanliness in all areas where food is stored, handled, prepared, and served. Invite the local health inspection people in as soon as you begin to lay out your renovation plans, and involve them in the early stages. What you want to avoid is costly eleventh-hour changes in the location of a kitchen drainpipe, for example. When the health department is involved early in the process, they have some "ownership" in the critical early decisions — and that helps!

The local fire department, wherever you are, has too few personnel and gets paid too little for what you and I expect it to do. That's a fairly broad statement, but if you consider the enormous responsibilities assigned to the fire and rescue people in America, I think you'll agree, they have an extraordinarily challenging assignment. You are about to be dealing with the local fire department quite differently than you have been as the tax-paying occupant of a single-family dwelling all these years. The fire safety aspects of a country inn are a matter of life and death — and they should be treated as such.

The placement of smoke alarms, sprinklers, fire doors, emergency exits, secure storage areas for flammable materials, designated smoking areas, and fire alarms are all potential areas of concern for your local fire safety officials. Just as you involve the health department in the early stages of your planning, you should keep the fire safety folks involved, too.

PUBLIC WORKS/TAXES/LICENSES

If you're like most aspiring innkeepers, you probably have not spent a lot of sleepless nights worrying about how many parking places you are going to have to provide for your country inn. That's fine, because the local public works and/or commercial licensing officials have already done it for you. Your team will come in handy once again in nailing down the specific requirements for paved parking and providing for safe and efficient entrances to and exits from the inn.

INSURANCE

The more you learn about the complexities of insuring your country inn, the more you will appreciate the suggestion made earlier in this book, that one of the key players on your professional management team be a well-trained insurance professional. As you will quickly see, your new insurance requirements differ widely from those of your personal insurance in terms of language, intent, and cost. Because of the growth of the industry in recent years, several insurance companies have developed special B&B and Country Inn package policies to help you achieve some economies of scale in your purchase. Arndt-McBee Insurance in Martinsburg, West Virginia (1-800-825-INNS), is one such company, and as you visit innkeepers you'll certainly learn of others.

As the owner/operator/proprietor of a country inn, you face a broad array of quite specific insurance requirements. Here is a brief checklist that will get you started in the right direction.

Liability

Minimum excess $5,000,000
Comprehensive personal liability
Business liability for country inn operations
Personal liability for owner-host
Product liability for food and beverage served
Premises medical for business guests
Premises medical for personal guests

Property

All Risk Coverage — Building
Replacement Cost on Building
All Risk / Named Peril Coverage on Contents
Replacement Cost Coverage on Contents
Appurtenant Structure Coverage / Business Related
Personal Property of Guests
Antiques and Fine Arts Coverage
Credit Card Coverage
Loss of Business Income (Business interruption) Coverage

Insurance is not just a "roll of the dice" for you or the insurer. As a commercial business it is very important that you now begin to think defensively. If you are dealing with the right insurance company, you will be pleased by how much effort they put into the area known as "risk management." Risk management essentially deals with all the operational details that can be integrated into your business to help you actually reduce risk. Such things as non-slip showers, ground fault interrupts on bathroom outlets, non-scald hot water monitors, and smoke alarms are all considered prudent components of a comprehensive risk-management program. Your insurance partner will apprise you of many others.

Chapter Seven

GETTING FINANCING

T he business plan and six-year financial projections you have just completed are the most important tool you have in securing financing for your new country inn. Not only is this business plan your own personal road map to financial success, it is clear evidence to anyone you approach for financial assistance that you have your feet firmly planted in reality and you are not shooting from the hip at an "off the wall" dream.

Your local banker may very well be your primary lender, and therefore it is important to make certain you have your financial act well rehearsed before you call upon him or her for assistance. Bankers are interested in some pretty basic, fundamental information. How much money do you seek . . . and for how long? What is the purpose of the loan? How do you plan to pay it back? What is the security you offer? All of the material you provide the bank supports and addresses one of these four points. Be prepared, be forthright, and be honest about your needs, and if your proposition has merit, you'll get the money you seek.

Be as specific in your business plan as possible. Your banker wants to know that you have identified the opportunities for improving the business and that you have a concrete plan for exploiting those opportunities. Do not attempt to articulate every operational detail of the business at this point. A carefully thought out restatement of your strategies for expanding the food service at the inn, including your plans for picnic lunches, brunches, private parties, high tea service, etc., and the projected impact of these ideas on the bottom line of the operation, are much more interesting for your banker than a laundry list of changes you plan to make in the overall operation.

Generally, any lender who considers backing your new venture is going to want to ensure that you are fully invested in the project personally. As you prepare your analysis of capital needs, make certain you have exhausted all your own personal possibilities prior to going to a third party. For example, if you have equity in your current residence, you will, in all likelihood, be applying those funds to your new country inn. If not . . . why? If you plan to live on the premises of your new inn, have your accountant and your attorney carefully review the tax laws relative to rolling over the gain in the sale of your primary residence into your inn. This can be a tricky area, so do not speculate. Get first-class professional advice on how to put the tax laws to work *for* you; otherwise you run the very real risk that the laws will work in exactly the opposite direction. Any other assets you (and your friends and family) have tucked away in your nest egg which may be considered sufficiently liquid to support your new venture should be indicated.

"When we liquidated our holdings in California, we netted around $1.2 million. It didn't take a rocket scientist to recognize that a project of this magnitude would probably drive us into the poor house. But given my lifelong philosophy of 'Hell, if they can do it, we can do it better!' we decided to proceed full steam ahead. The $1.2 million was swallowed up so quickly we were amazed.

"Our plan from the beginning was to return these two gorgeous Southern mansions to their original 1868 splendor . . . with one significant exception. We doubted that we could succeed as an inn if our guests all had to share the same bathroom, or if we didn't have adequate heating and air conditioning throughout the property. Consequently, we had to upgrade the power and plumbing from their meager 1868 functional utility to serve a modern-day inn operation. Since we had never done this before, we had no earthly idea of the costs and expenses involved in a project of this magnitude.

"Once our $1.2 million was gone, we realized we had clearly come too far to quit, so we borrowed an additional $900,000 to finish what we had started. As I said earlier, we had no intentions of just shuffling off into the typical life of retirement. Investing a couple of million dollars in a new business with zero guarantee of success was perhaps even further removed from that typical retirement than we could ever have imagined. So we were off and running — with a brand new mortgage to prove it!

"We had reasoned that our kids were all grown and this would be a lot more fun than plopping our money into a CD somewhere — and we were right. This experience has been fabulous. If I had known how wonderful this hospitality business really is, I would have been in it forty years ago. It has taken us almost a lifetime to find where we belong — and innkeeping is it."

Also, be sure as you begin your capital-raising effort that you look into the several federally funded, low-interest loan programs that might apply to your situation. For instance, if you are acquiring a historic structure, there may very well be low-interest rehabilitation funding available at particularly attractive rates and terms. Similarly, your local community development office may have block grant funds or similar programs that encourage the recycling of important one-of-a-kind structures. Your banker, your real-estate adviser, and your lawyer should be able to help you in identifying these.

Next, consider the possibility of a second mortgage on the inn property, or a short-term revolving loan at the prevailing rate of interest. As you deal with suppliers, look for terms of payment that meet your needs. In the early months and years of your operation, it is a good idea to hang on to as much of your actual cash resources as possible. You are going to need them sooner or later. If one of your equipment suppliers is in a position to extend particularly attractive payment terms and another supplier is not, you might prefer to do business with the company where your financial resources go the furthest.

"Our smartest investments in the business were, first of all and most importantly, the addition of staff. For us, that was a very costly, but extremely important early lesson. It's much easier, frankly, to just prepare the dinner with a few helpers and serve it ourselves, but as the volume of business expanded that simply was no longer possible and we had to bring in the right people at the right time.

"The second important investment we made was the money we invested to expand the business. We began the inn with six rooms and quickly added a seventh. Two years later we added three more. The expansion to ten guest rooms was the turning point in our business — and the point where our operation began to return a consistent profit — in spite of the fact that we had to borrow the money for the leasehold improvements.

"The third most important investment we made in our business was an investment we had not planned, and looking back it is astounding that we debated the decision so long. I can't imagine running the business now without a computer. Any aspiring innkeeper who thinks it might be possible to get along without a computer is simply not facing reality. Although we're certainly not afraid to work, we had set out a general game plan for how best we preferred to spend our time and talents, and housekeeping and cooking were not high on that agenda."

One of the charming bedrooms in the Inn at Sawmill Farm, West Dover, Vermont.

Chapter Eight

THE RESTAURANT BUSINESS

Planning

Preparation

Presentation

Food Service Cost Accounting

One of the vital points of differentiation for a country inn is the food and beverage side of the business. Many highly successful country inns merchandise their facilities as MAP, or Modified American Plan, which essentially means dinner is included along with breakfast in the overnight room rate. If you or your partner have not had previous experience in the restaurant business, at a bare minimum hire a food and beverage consultant, preferably an experienced innkeeper, who can teach you some of the fundamentals.

Some of innkeeping's most successful partnerships have survived over time because one of the partners concentrated his or her primary energies on the food and beverage side of the inn and the other partner concentrated on the rest of the operation. That doesn't mean the roles were never reversed or shared, but when one person is responsible for the clearly defined area of the kitchen, generally everything will run a lot more smoothly.

"I really love challenging myself in our kitchen and our successes in the fine dining side of our operation have played a major role in our success. I feel confident our dining facilities made it possible for us to earn the Mobil 4 Star rating, and to maintain a consistently strong reputation for creative, healthful, and interesting cuisine. Our guest rooms are lovely, but small. Without our dining facilities, we would be a completely different kind of business — and I don't think it would nearly as much fun."

Three separate and distinct food and beverage service opportunities exist in a country inn — breakfast, afternoon tea, and dinner. These services may of course be augmented by the sale of picnics, box lunches, etc., and food and beverage may be incorporated into other parts of the day. For example, at the Clifton Inn in Charlottesville, Virginia, a time-honored tradition and guest favorite is the bottomless cookie jar, kept full of freshly baked cookies, which the guests may enjoy at any time, day or night. In addition, the Clifton maintains a supply of complimentary beverages in a small refrigerator, and their guests are invited to serve themselves at any time.

These two examples of complimentary extras or *lagniappes* must be considered part of the food and beverage planning of a typical country inn. That is to say, when you are planning your overall food and beverage costs, make certain to include the cost of those products in your accounting.

Operating a country inn kitchen involves the three "P's": planning, preparation, and presentation.

PLANNING

Each week, the person responsible for the operation of the inn kitchen must prepare a careful projection of the menus for the week, including not only what will be served, but in what quantities (based on reservations in-house), and what raw materials (grocery list) are necessary to prepare them. This planning process becomes particularly important where the purchase of perishables is concerned, and even more critical when the distance between the market and the inn is a considerable one. As a rule, successful country inns invariably settle upon a handful of consistently good, reasonably easily prepared breakfast and dinner items that can be rotated.

PREPARATION

If you've ever planned a dinner party for eight or ten couples, you already know how challenging the chopping, slicing, and dicing can be. In the well-organized country inn kitchen, it is not unusual for the tedious and time-consuming "prep" chores to be assigned to an hourly employee, trainee, or assistant chef.

Familiarity with the menu enables many of the preparation steps to be performed well in advance in order to cut down on the crisis kitchen syndrome. If fresh-baked cookies, muffins, and breads are featured in your inn, they too can be scheduled for production in such a manner as to avoid a direct conflict with the meal service.

PRESENTATION

Maybe it's just an exercise in semantics to some people, but not to the dedicated country innkeeper: you may "serve" your family their dinner at home, but you "present" dinner to your guests at the inn. Every country inn has a unique routine that suits the personalities of the innkeepers and the tone of the facility. At the Gastonian, Hugh Lineberger banters with the guests while he pours their fresh-squeezed juice. This breaks the ice, and before long the guests are engaging in relaxed comfortable dialogue with the other guests at the table. At the Inn of the Animal Tracks in Santa Fe, each table is set with earthenware glazed with the footprints of a different animal. The guests invariably begin their meals with a light-hearted exchange among themselves about the theme of the inn.

Some innkeepers actually come into the dining room and announce the evening's menu. You'll find your own comfort level and a sense of informality or formality appropriate to your facility.

The presentation of each meal service at your inn is an important part of the signature of your facility. One of the Grant Corner Inn's signature food items is, quite appropriately, a Southwestern garnish Pat prepares by using a saguarro cactus-shaped cookie cutter to slice out cactus-shaped pieces of the native root vegetable jicama. He then soaks the jicama in a bright green mint-flavored solution which adds color and cool mint flavor to whatever dish being served — and he has created a Grant Corner original idea the guest will always recall.

FOOD SERVICE COST ACCOUNTING

Some innkeepers choose to group their food and beverage opera-tions into their overall inn revenues and expenses. If, however, you are interested in maintaining a firm handle on the various segments of your operation, it is essential that you produce a separate financial report for the food and beverage side of your operation, complete with all related expenses. Simply knowing that industry averages for food cost run between 35 and 45 percent of sales is not enough.

One very helpful resource for the innkeeper/restaurateur is the Na-tional Restaurant Association in Washington D.C. The NRA offers a variety of reference and member support information, in addition to hosting one of the largest annual exhibitions in the country. *Nation's Restaurant News,* published by Lebhar Friedman, Inc., in New York City, is a helpful weekly publication that provides its readers with a good overall sense of the food and beverage industry.

Picnic Baskets

Question: How can you increase your revenue per guest room without increasing the price of the room or the price of any meal served in your dining room, and do so without investing a lot of capital? One increasingly popular way is to offer a picnic basket to your overnight guest. Most successful country inns that offer picnic baskets adhere to a couple of basic principles:

1. Be sure to make the guest aware of the picnic basket through a tastefully executed table tent or blackboard that describes the contents of the basket and its cost.

2. Create a picnic basket menu that is based on seasonally available ingredients and requires minimal preparation time.

3. Price the picnic basket competitively by maintaining a 30 to 35 percent cost of goods. For example, if your picnic basket for two contains a selection of salads, breads, pâté, fresh fruit, cheese, and a bottle of wine or champagne, and the total cost of the ingredients is $15, the retail price of the picnic basket would be $50 at a food cost of 30 percent, or $43 if you maintain a 35 percent food cost.

4. Prepare a "picnic map" that directs your guests to a romantic setting for their dining adventure.

5. Invest in a picnic basket set containing high-quality unbreakable tableware, and have a local artist paint your inn's logo on the lid.

Chapter Nine

COMPUTERS IN THE INN

"Our smartest investment in the business, over and above our substantial renovation, was purchasing a computer and shifting all our accounting functions over to it. We have also incorporated all our mailing list, marketing, and front desk functions into our computer program. Previously the inn did not have a computer, so it was severely limited in the type of direct mailings it could do, for example. In addition, since our predecessors had to use an outside bookkeeper and accountant for handling payroll and financial report generation, there was a sizable added expense. Computerizing those functions enabled us to eliminate those expenses for the outside vendors and to increase the quality and efficiency of our own systems at the same time."

In this day and age, even an inn of six or eight rooms should be computer-based in its accounting and marketing functions. The National Restaurant Association offers a variety of easy-to-use software programs to serve the food service side of the country inn. The front desk functions such as reservations, confirmations, daily journal entries, etc., are also supported by dozens of popular and inexpensive programs. Pal and MacInn for the IBM and Macintosh respectively are both highly recommended, essential tools for operating a contemporary country inn.

As computers have grown to play an increasingly vital role in the day-to-day operations of country inns all over America, a variety of software-savvy individuals and companies have come upon the scene to serve the innkeeper. The following summary of computer software providers has been compiled by Inn Marketing Yellow Pages, P.O. Box 1789, Kankakee, IL 60901.

Action Pacific Software, P.O. Box 1634, Hamilton MT 59849, 406-363-6528 — IBM Compatible software programs for innkeepers

Bed & Breakfast of Rhode Island, Box 3291, Newport, RI 02840, 401-849-1298 — Information for reservation services

B&B Rocky Mtns., Box 804, Colorado Springs, CO 80901, 719-630-3433 — Software to organize host/guest activities

CAPA Software Publishing, 211-3521 8th St., Saskatoon, Canada 37H-OW5 — Management package for front desk and accounting

Doolittle Services, Inc., Box 350, Barneveld, NY 13304, 315-896-4607

Eliot Software, Box 338, Eliot, ME 03903, 207-439-9361

The Front Desk, Box 1706, Guerneville, CA 95446, 707-869-3121
IBM compatible reservation, billing, guest history, and list management

InnSoft, 3421 23rd Ave. S., Minneapolis, MN 55407, 612-724-7846
Inn management software

MacInn Software, Box 216, Eliot, ME 03903, 207-439-9361
Front Desk and Reservation system

MicroPlan Systems, 100 Galli Dr., Novato, CA 94949, 800-537-5274
Personalized record keeping for the lodging industry

Mullberry Computers, Box 2247, Mission Viejo, CA 92690,
800-999-1995 — Reservation and tax system

Pal Computers, Box 790, Manchester Ctr., VT 05255, 802-362-2227
Comprehensive computer program for country inns

The Salem Inn, 7 Summer St., Salem, MA 01970, 508-741-0680
Software for innkeepers

Softserv Computer Services, 7915 FM 1960 W, #226, Houston,
TX 77070 — IBM compatible software for small inns and hotels

Note: The Professional Association of Innkeepers International, P.O. Box
90710, Santa Barbara, CA 93190 (FAX: 805-682-1016), offers a set of ten
thoroughly tested inn-specific programs at a very nominal charge.

Once again, make it a point to ask the innkeepers you visit about
their own personal preferences in computer support hardware and software. The old adage about "ask the man who owns one" applies here
in spades! You'll learn more in a ten-minute exchange with an innkeeper who uses a computer in the day-to-day business than you could
learn in this book or any other. Bear in mind that each inn is different.
Do not begin by buying the next computer you see on sale at your
neighborhood computer store. Take the time to analyze the type of

business you are going to be running, including the number of guest rooms, payroll, food and beverage operations, etc., and select the equipment that matches your needs. Often your accountant can provide some insight into other similar businesses and the programs they have selected and use with success.

"When we acquired the inn, we also acquired our predecessor's standing monthly contract with an outside bookkeeping service. They were preparing their monthly recaps and sending them to the service. Thirty days later the service returned a financial statement for the period. As it worked out, the innkeepers were paying $300 dollars each month for a financial statement which would generally arrive six weeks after the close of the period in question. We installed our own accounting program at a one-time program acquisition cost of $150. Now we have our P&L statements literally on a daily basis. We're producing much more timely information with which to make our management decisions, and we're saving a considerable amount of money at the same time."

When these same innkeepers discovered their predecessors were also sending out their payroll every two weeks at a cost of $50 each time, they analyzed the payroll. They immediately realized that most of the work being done on the payroll, such as calculation of tip credits and total hours worked, was actually being done at the inn first, and then phoned into the payroll service. The payroll service would in turn write the individual checks, and the inn would hand-deliver a master payroll check including the $50 charge, pick up the payroll checks, and return to the inn for distribution to the employees. With their new computer program up and running, the innkeepers were able to completely eliminate the payroll service and move the entire process "in-house." The end result: *"We save not only the $1,300 in fees each year, but we have a much more efficient system of internal payroll controls."*

In addition to the added relevance and increased utility of concise and timely revenue and expense reports, it's important to realize that solid and accurate computer-generated financial statements become one of the most important assets you can have if and when you decide to sell your inn.

Judd and Susan Levy in front of the Vermont Inn, Killington, Vermont.

Chapter Ten

PULLING IT ALL TOGETHER
AND OPENING THE DOOR

Associations and Start-Ups

Start-Up Slip-Ups

If You Remember Only One Thing . . .

ASSOCIATIONS AND START-UPS

Opening your country inn may be among the most interesting challenges of your professional life, but it certainly need not be a lonely one. Local, regional, and national support groups can be an important network of support for the new country innkeeper. Although the degree to which you accept or decline the good counsel of these various organizations is completely up to you, plan now to explore in depth how best this industry's infrastructure might help you.

The list of human resources available to help you get opened invariably starts with those who have been there before you. Here are a few of the comments from around the table about those bewildering early days of keeping the inn.

"In the early days, there was a lot of competition among the innkeepers. As the industry has matured, it seems the innkeepers are working together more in the best interests of serving people. The B&B Innkeepers of Northern California was our first association experience and we've subsequently been fortunate to be invited to join a number of professional associations such as the Independent Innkeeper's Association." Although the Carter House has been voted Inn of the Year, and has consistently been among the top inns in the nation, they have learned that by constantly trying to make people happy and do the best job possible every day, the awards and special recognitions will pretty much take care of themselves.

Some of the various industry support groups and organizations will be more beneficial to the new innkeeper than others. Take the time to thoroughly research the organizations, newsletters, and workshops listed throughout this book. As a prospective innkeeper, you'll find the associations and consultants who concentrate on industry fundamentals, start-ups, and property valuation most helpful at the outset. Over time, as you and your inn begin to mature in the industry, the associations whose members most closely reflect your inn's size and marketing thrust will have greater value to you and your business. The Linebergers, innkeepers and owners of the Gastonian in Savannah, belong to only one professional organization, and for them that works well.

"In the seven years we've been open, we've seen a veritable flock of inn-specific publications and guidebooks arrive on the scene. We are members of one and only one professional support group, the Independent Innkeeper's Association. We think this organization is

*more consistent with our own philosophy of doing business than
some of the others which are out there. All our members must own
and operate our own properties and be subject to regular and strin-
gent inspections of the property. Our inspections have a zero-toler-
ance factor. Our members either pass or fail."*

When you mention inns in America many people automatically think
of Vermont. Throughout New England many proud and venerable buildings are enjoying an elegant renaissance at the hands of some very
talented and dedicated innkeepers. One such inn is the Governor's Inn.
Listen as Deedy Marble describes their professional affiliations.

*"We are members of both the Independent Innkeeper's Associa-
tion and the Professional Association of Innkeepers International. I
am personally very impressed with PAII, which is an extremely professional and helpful organization particularly for the smaller keepers of inns. They provide a lot of support and guidance for innkeepers and a great forum for the exchange of ideas between other
members of this great fraternity. In my opinion the IIA is a bit more
oriented to the more seasoned and established innkeepers who maybe
don't require quite as much handholding and TLC."*

Joyce and Jim Acton, former innkeepers of the White Oak Inn in
Ohio, had a somewhat different outlook on how they worked with their
various support groups. Like a lot of innkeeping partners, the Actons
found it economically sensible for Jim to continue working at his corporate position in the city while Joyce concentrated her full-time energies
on the inn. As a result of his professional association with the community, he found himself on the board of directors of the chamber of
commerce and United Way, which were extremely helpful in gaining
visibility for the inn.

Jim carried the local involvement further than most new innkeepers
when he accepted a position as the paid executive director of the local
chamber of commerce for a year and a half, prior to joining Joyce in the
inn full-time. Although that level of involvement is not possible for all
innkeepers, it is interesting to observe the impact it had on getting the
inn noticed early and effectively. Jim's activities at the chamber were a
big help in getting the White Oak established in the local community.

Judd Levy found the investment of time and effort he and his wife
Susan made in the area around the Vermont Inn to be a rewarding one.

"We are members of PAII and we still attend a Bill Oates seminar each year, but other than that we have little time for the other professional groups and meetings. I am active as a board member of one of our local trade groups, and I have been active in helping to develop promotional ideas for our area. That local involvement has had a noticeable effect on our restaurant and referral business."

START-UP SLIP-UPS

Perhaps one of the most common pitfalls for the new innkeeper is the tendency to assume automatically that because the innkeeper likes it, the guest will like it. While considerable effort has been expended throughout this book discussing the importance of the innkeepers being themselves, and imprinting the business with their own taste and touches, it's probably a good idea to keep in mind the old adage about moderation in all things.

"When we first started in this business, we would buy every cutesy little 'inn-looking' decorative accessory we came across. Inevitably a day or two later it would break, or its mate would break, and we'd move it into our basement, which has become the final resting place for all those cute little personal things we simply could not live without. All the personal little treasures like Granny's antique quilt or that wonderful tea set are all motivated by the right emotion — but the wrong reality!"

Instead of enhancing the guest's experience, you'll find that quite often the guest is uncomfortable or even actually intimidated by certain kinds of obviously one-of-a-kind personal treasures. As you prepare to furnish your inn, you need to find that wonderful balance between serviceable elegance and individuality. It's got to be comfortable and utilitarian enough that the guest feels at home and not constantly in fear of damaging something irreplaceable. As Louise Stewart explains, some of the most valuable lessons in the innkeeping business will often come directly from the guests themselves.

"Room 9 was the first guest room we rented after opening, to a lovely Canadian couple. I had proudly furnished this room with one of my real family treasures, my mother's antique table, which I value

so much I guard it with my life. I naturally assumed that this couple would appreciate this table as much as we did. As it worked out, the table was actually in the way. The couple came to me the morning after their first night and asked, somewhat sheepishly, if it would be possible to move the table so they would have room for their own luggage and other personal effects."

Room 11 in the Grant Corner Inn used to be Bumpy's bedroom. *"When we made it into a guest room we decided to theme the room around our daughter's dolls and stuffed animals. The reason this idea worked for Room 11 is we had a tall shelf when went around the room and provided a perfect place to display the toys. It gives the room a unique flavor without getting in the guest's way."*

One of the favorite personal touches in a well-appointed country inn is the family pictures of some of the original inn occupants, which are often displayed on the walls in the foyer and parlor. Once again, these "before" shots are wonderful thematic touches that can be thoroughly enjoyed by the guest without getting in the way. But a universal inngoer pet peeve is the innkeepers who insist upon displaying the collection of silver framed photos on the night stand, cluttering it so completely that there is no room left for the guest to place his or her own reading glasses and reading material.

Another commonly heard pet peeve concerns lighting. The typical inn guest enjoys reading, and often prefers it to the standard 21-inch color television with the remote control. That said, why do so many inns refuse to provide strong and effective reading lights in their guest rooms? Inns take great pains to provide timely and current reading material on the night stand beside the bed — with very little light by which to read it.

Innkeepers without a sense of humor simply do not exist. Jim and Joyce Acton's knack for seeing the humor in much of their day-to-day innkeeping made it possible for them to start from nothing and create a successful country inn. Having sold their business, the Actons bring a unique perspective to the roundtable. At a personal level, Joyce appreciated most the creative challenges of furnishing and decorating the inn and operating the kitchen. *"I discovered that I really do love cooking . . . and that love of working in the kitchen ultimately became an important part of our marketing mix. We learned quickly that people were seeking out the inn for our meal service."*

At the outset, the Actons began operation as a classic bed and breakfast inn. Because of their somewhat remote and off-the-beaten-track location, they quickly realized that inn guests were not eager, after checking in and getting comfortable, to climb back in their car for a trip to the nearest decent restaurant. Once the guests curl up next to the fire during the winter or settle with an ice-cold lemonade into their favorite rocking chair on the porch during the summer, the last thing they want to do is leave the comfort of their inn for dinner.

As a result, and as an operating necessity, Joyce discovered she had a genuine knack for preparing well-received dinners. *"I consider it kind of a gift . . . a skill I honestly did not know I possessed, until we had to call upon it as part of being in the inn business. I also consider it to be a gift which I have grown to love sharing with others."*

While busy promoting the tourism throughout Northern California Mark Carter is careful to keep his innkeeping shoes firmly on the ground.

"For the new innkeeper the barrier to entry into this industry is greater today than ten years ago in most major markets," Mark explains, *"but the fundamentals of this business do not change."* Mark sums up the fundamentals this way:

"We are still in the business of serving people. My wife or I make it a point to be at the door to greet our guests when they first arrive and when they depart. People appreciate this kind of personalized hospitality, especially in an increasingly mechanized and computerized society.

"When our guests depart and compliment us we have a three word sentence which is the central theme of our marketing program — TELL A FRIEND! As simple as that may sound, it is the favorable word-of-mouth that is the least expensive and most effective form of marketing and advertising we can have. Unfortunately, that saw cuts both ways. If a guest has a less than positive experience, they'll share that with their friends and neighbors too."

Judd Levy gives us an excellent example of the process of constantly evolving marketing priorities.

"Let me give you an example of some of the kinds of choices you'll face with regard to how you position your property for the long haul. We are proud of the fact that we have a three-diamond restaurant operation here at the Vermont Inn. We've been told by the folks who are responsible for the ratings that we are serving a quality of

food that could easily earn us a fourth diamond IF (AND ONLY IF) we'd be willing to make a 'few changes' in the inn.

"Those changes would include new uniforms for our staff, completely new china and glassware, removing six or seven of our twenty tables from the dining room, putting down new carpeting in the dining room, redoing our ceiling, and essentially completely changing the nature of our dining room. The point I am making here, is we feel because of the type of property we have chosen to operate, and the type of business we have created, we would much prefer to own and operate a profitable three-diamond property than an unprofitable four-diamond inn."

All too often, in this business, people aspire to unreasonable and potentially counterproductive levels of success, as defined by someone else. The real challenge is to identify the optimal level of success and visibility for your business while understanding that elevating your own visibility or adding another diamond for your inn might come at a very real cost. Whether it is a hard cash cost, like buying new china and glassware, or merely the cost of diverting your time away from the day-to-day business, there is indeed a measurable trade-off.

IF YOU REMEMBER ONLY ONE THING . . .

No matter how much money you project you'll need to get your inn up and running, YOU'RE ALWAYS GOING TO NEED MORE. From the only former investment banker on our roundtable: *"As an investment banker on Wall Street for the ten years immediately preceding our entry into the inn business, I felt I had a fairly good understanding of what it took to run a business. Although my financial and business background was helpful to us, we still dramatically underestimated how much cash the business would consume in the early days. Contingency funds are always going to be depleted. If it's not the furnace it's a pipe that freezes and breaks."*

Without a doubt, the most common and potentially most hazardous mistake made by a fledgling innkeeper is to purchase a new property and not have sufficient funds in reserve to support the unexpected decline in business that radically reduces revenues, or that extraordinary event which exponentially raises expenses. It cannot be emphasized enough that you should have either a prearranged line of credit at the bank or sufficient cash on hand to allow for unforeseen circumstances.

Budgets must be prepared on an annual basis and should reflect the month-in and month-out realities of the business. Monthly financial statements are a fact of life. They should be reviewed immediately upon their completion and in minute detail to make certain that any areas of the business that are out of line are identified and corrected without causing further financial damage to the business.

Now that you've come this far, you've practically finished the start-up procedures for opening your inn. But before you go any further, you'll need to consider how to spread the word about your new establishment. No doubt you will have pondered this already; it is an ongoing task, to be carried out before, during, and long after you open your doors.

In the next chapter, we'll take up some marketing strategies that are important for the new innkeeper.

The gazebo is featured in promotional photographs from the Barrows House, Dorset, Vermont.

Chapter Eleven

MARKETING YOUR INN

Naming and Theming Your Inn

Developing a Logo

Setting Your Room Rates

Levels of Occupancy

Identifying Your Guest

One of the most critical but least understood prerequisites for opening a country inn is a well-orchestrated and properly executed marketing program. The higher-profile successful innkeepers, and the ones to whom all the rest turn for advice and counsel, inevitably fall into one of two categories. They are either "old pros" in the field of marketing, or they are seasoned veterans of the innkeeping business who have combined their own natural skills of communication with a predominantly self-taught marketing strategy. There are important lessons to be learned from both.

You'll often hear the three terms marketing, advertising, and public relations tossed about as though they were interchangeable. That's not the case; each has its own meaning and purpose. The marketing function — so essential to opening your inn — will be discussed here; advertising and promotion will be covered in Part Three.

Marketing is defined by the American Marketing Association as "the process of planning and executing the conception, pricing, promotion, and distribution of ideas, goods, and services to create exchanges that satisfy individual and organizational objectives." When applied to innkeeping, marketing includes everything from creating the name and graphic identity of the inn to setting the price structure for the guest rooms to buying a newspaper ad that promotes Sunday brunch.

In essence, marketing consists of all the activities that bring the buyers (your guests) and the sellers (you) together. You've heard of the "offer you can't refuse"; the goal of the innkeeper's marketing plan should be to create such an attractive and unique selling proposition that the guest is compelled to pick up the telephone and book a weekend visit.

NAMING AND THEMING YOUR INN

Much has been written about the need for a gimmick or angle that attracts guests' attention just long enough for them to read more about your facility — to "buy into" your selling proposition. In reality, this will grow quite naturally from the theme you choose for your property. Do not let the task of identifying a theme overwhelm you. You are surrounded by terrific stepping-off points from which your inn's identity might evolve.

As you research the industry and learn more about successful inns, you'll realize that the most frequent thematic anchor for a country inn in America is undoubtedly the inn's own history. If you are acquiring a structure that has never been operated as an inn, then you might wish to research the backgrounds of the building and its prior owners, and develop a theme from that point forward.

Other natural themes arise from the physical properties of the structure and the grounds it occupies. For example, there is a lot to be said for naming your structure after, and thematically anchoring your inn on, the beautiful century-old oak trees in the front yard. When those oak trees are identified as among the oldest in the community and they have been loved by generations of local residents, naming your inn "The Oaks," as Tom and Elizabeth Ray did in Christiansburg, Virginia, can win you a lot of praise and some important public relations kudos at the same time.

Your research into your building's history may turn up wonderful revelations such as that it once housed a notorious gang of train robbers — or the finest bordello west of the Mississippi River! That's colorful stuff to talk about over hot chocolate on the porch, but it doesn't readily lend itself to adoption as a theme for the property. What should you do?

Create a theme that mirrors you. If photography is your lifelong passion, or doll collecting, or century-old tableware — go for it! You'll be astounded at how many terrific ways you'll be able to integrate your own hobbies, tastes, and passions into your inn.

The more you brainstorm the possibilities, the closer you'll be to settling on the perfect name. And once you've picked the name of your inn, it's time to select a logo for the property. Developing a compelling graphic identity for your inn should be among your early initiatives.

DEVELOPING A LOGO

If you are short on funds, then contact the local community college art department and offer to sponsor a design contest. The winning design will earn for its creator an all-expenses-paid weekend at the inn. However you manage it, do not spend even ten dollars on something as simple as a one-page fact sheet or a press release before you decide on the permanent name and logo for your inn.

At this point in the development of your inn's identity, it's important that you be thinking of the long term. A little common sense in the evaluation of an appropriate logo will go a long way. As you consider all the places a logo might be used, from letterhead and press kit to tiny one-column one- or-two-inch display ads in the back of a national or regional lifestyle magazine, you will realize that your logo must be not only clever, but clear and readable as well. Generally, a logo that is slightly wider than a perfect square will work well in virtually all applications.

Recent advancements in desktop publishing, and the availability of a broad array of attractive type styles and sizes, now make it possible for anyone with a basic desktop PC or Apple computer to design and produce a quite functional logo. If you also have access to a laser printer, you can crank out camera-ready graphics at a fraction of the costs without even involving the local typesetter and printer.

Once your logo is complete, have your artist and/or typesetter produce several sheets of logos in various sizes. By always maintaining a file of camera-ready logos you will be able to ensure consistency in your graphic identity throughout the early development stages of your property. When an advertising opportunity arises, or you need to have a new sign painted, you'll be prepared!

SETTING YOUR ROOM RATES

Although the price structure you set for your inn might seem part of administration, not marketing, it may well be the most important marketing decision you make in the early stages of your operation. Marketing, as we said earlier, consists of all the activities that bring buyers and sellers together. Certainly the rate you ask for your guest rooms will be central to whether a guest chooses to stay with you or at some other facility nearby.

It's research time. Since your inn will not be operating in a vacuum, you cannot set the room rates arbitrarily. Prior to establishing your rates, make it your business to know everyone else's. Since you are not open yet, and all the other lodging and dining facilities are, you can have the advantage of knowing exactly how they are handling rates, promotions, and packages. This can be an important competitive edge for your operation.

Set your rate with one eye on the market and one idea on your own operating reality. For example, you could find yourself perfectly positioned with your rate approach, relative to the market around you, and still end up a financial failure because your occupancy levels fail to generate sufficient cash income to fully service your debt and meet the costs of running the   business.   That said, let's take a look, from a marketing perspective, on how to arrive at a competitively successful room rate.

First, contact the local chamber of commerce, convention and visitors council, and the other community development specialists in your area and determine the overall levels of hotel and motel occupancy. Next, call all the hotels, motels, guest houses, and inns in your community and request their current brochures, promotional packets, and room rates. If you are in an area that caters to a seasonal business, be sure to request the rate information for both the high and the low seasons.

As your file of local information grows, organize the lodging facilities in your area into a prioritized list beginning with your primary competition and continuing on down the list through your secondary and tertiary competitors. Alternatively, you can rate the facilities from most to least expensive, and see where your facility falls in the hierarchy.

This categorizing will accomplish several important goals for you. First, you will begin more clearly to understand your competitive environment. By doing this you will also identify where your primary customers are now.

Next, give some of your friends the list, along with a narrative of what your new inn will offer. Ask them to rate the existing facilities from best to worst, and to judge which facilities they believe might offer the stiffest competition.

Although some facilities in your area, such as the moderately upscale, 100-plus guest room chains, may command rates similar to yours, they might not be ideal for comparison. If the local larger hotels cater primarily to groups, you will not even be in the running for their primary stream of business. On the other hand, if there is a six-year-old country inn on the other side of town, with the same number of guest rooms as your new facility and a generally comparable amenity package, you should carefully observe their rate structure and price your facilities accordingly.

Once you have determined where your new inn fits in the local market, including food, beverage, amenities, location, number of guest rooms, etc., you will have an excellent grasp of the nightly room rate the market can support.

For example, let's assume the competitive environment rate analysis reveals a $34.95 per night budget motel on the outskirts of town, a $45 per night B&B five miles from town with shared baths, a Holiday Inn with a commercial rate of $53, a Hyatt with a standard rate of $90, and a Marriott resort twelve miles away by the interstate, which charges $145 to $290 per night. After thoroughly analyzing what the local overnight guest is getting for the money, you might determine that with your breakfast included, all private baths, complimentary tea in the afternoon, evening brandy, and bed linen turndown service, the market will welcome you at $85 per night.

LEVELS OF OCCUPANCY

Now that you are beginning to grasp the local rate structure, it's time to turn your other eye to the year-round levels of occupancy that prevail in the area. Although there is a variety of ways to weight competitive facilities based upon their projected direct impact on your business, in projecting occupancy levels, two words of advice should prevail: be conservative.

The Professional Association of Innkeepers International (PAII) strongly urges a phased-in approach to establishing occupancy projections, which begin in the first year with the inn projected at half the local going rate of occupancy. For example, if the local chamber and tourism folks tell you the year-round occupancy rate for all lodging facilities in your area is 70 percent, you would project your first year's occupancy rate at 35 percent. In subsequent years, remember the PAII recommendation to be conservative and add an additional 10 percent per year. Returning to our example, Year Two would be 45 percent and Year Three, 55 percent occupancy.

You may of course use any combination of formulas you wish in order to arrive at your own occupancy projections. For example, it may be much more important to you to know the levels of occupancy of the facility in your market whose rates are closest to what you are planning to charge, rather than an overall occupancy projection for the entire market. If those occupancy rates are dramatically different from the overall market, they might be a better barometer of your own occupancy. Whichever method you choose, by always being as conservative as possible you can avoid entering the business with unrealistic expectations.

IDENTIFYING YOUR GUESTS

Now that we've named our facility, designed our logo, and generally determined where we're headed in terms of rates and guest counts, let's address a few of the many other factors which will play a role in our marketing efforts. It is not possible even to consider an ongoing advertising or public relations effort without having a clear picture of the person we plan to serve.

A lot of what you need to know about your projected target guest has already been determined for you. Based on the phenomenal growth of innkeeping, and the ever-increasing professionalism at all levels of the business, we have begun to understand the inn guest better. We now know that the majority of inn guests are college-educated married couples between the ages of thirty-five and fifty-four, with annual household incomes in excess of $50,000. We also know that a substantial number of inn guests are either "empty nesters" with no school-age children remaining at home, or "DINKS" (Double Income, No Kids).

These affluent, well-educated consumers are mobile, curious, and somewhat adventurous, and they visit an inn more often than not because a friend, co-worker, or neighbor recommended the facility. Other than guidebooks, which account for some 85 percent of visits, word of mouth is the most common factor (in more than 80 percent of the cases) influencing the decision to visit a particular country inn.

Although in recent years the number of inn guests who are traveling on business has increased, people still visit an inn most often for pleasure. Based on numerous studies and questionnaires over the past few years, we know the single most important factor in an inn experience is the hospitality of the innkeeper. Breakfast, as part of the package, and private baths are also critical factors in the minds of inngoers.

As innkeeping has blossomed into a marketing and entrepreneurial success story, the marketplace has responded in kind. Several mid- and upscale chain hotel operations have begun incorporating a complimentary breakfast into their overnight lodging packages. Positive consumer response has even urged some chain properties to offer at-cost or complimentary high tea and/or happy hour as further enticements to attract overnight business.

Not to be outdone, innkeepers have begun to blur the lines between country inns and the upscale chains that offer a seemingly endless array of amenities. Ten years ago it was considered progressive if an inn had private baths with all guest rooms.   Today, as the above research points out, it is virtually a necessity to the more discerning and demanding inn guest. Likewise, toll-free reservation numbers, private telephones, fax machines, and even in-room VCRs are rapidly finding a home in the inn. Scented soaps, designer shampoos, private-label wines, and custom-molded chocolate candies have also become a common part of the sophisticated country inn's hospitality package.

With a basic understanding of the inngoer and what he or she seeks in an inn experience, you can begin focusing more closely on the target guest in your particular market. Take a look around your community. When the visitors who fit the inngoer profile come to your town, where do they stay? What do they do during their visit? What time of the year do they generally visit? Where do they come from? How long are they in town? Quite often, the more you learn, the clearer the strategy for reaching these people will become.

> One roundtable member observed that the local university was considered to be quite a plus when they did the initial market feasibility study. Alumni functions, athletic events, concerts, plays, etc., were all natural attractions that suggested potential inn business. It was only after better understanding the travel patterns in and around the town that they noticed a huge, previously unidentified marketing opportunity.
>
> The student recruiting office at the university had never been approached by a lodging facility of any kind, much less an inn. The university staff was only too pleased to provide the inn with their mailing list of prospective students. In exchange, the inn offered a special rate package to visiting prospective students and their families. Presto! One of the inn's most important midweek business marketing concepts was born and continues as part of the business today.

Now that you have pretty well completed the steps necessary for opening your inn and have developed some marketing strategies, you're ready to tackle the challenges of daily operations. In fact, you probably have already done much work in this area, because the line between *opening* an inn and *operating* it is not hard and fast: in truth, the work of getting started blends imperceptibly into the task of running your operation.

In Part Three, we'll take a closer look at daily operations. As a part of this exercise, we'll have the opportunity, from time to time, to take extended looks "behind the curtains" of successful operations, listening to the owners describe their typical day and their many tasks. To put you in the mood, here's one such look at the work of Judd and Susan Levy, innkeepers whose insights have not only contributed much to the roundtable discussions but also have helped to shape the financial information.

Behind the Curtains . . .
The Vermont Inn, Killington, Vermont • Judd and Susan Levy.

The Levys keep the Vermont Inn, joined by their daughters, Elissa and Jennifer, during the busy season. The inn is an 1840 farmhouse that has been lovingly restored and renovated to house a nineteen-room country inn. It has been in operation as a lodge or inn for nearly half a century. Fifteen of the guest rooms have private baths, and four share two large hall baths. The very success-ful fifty-seat restaurant in the Vermont Inn serves the public as well as the inn's MAP guests.

Killington has worked diligently to create a year-round recre-ational environment which now includes craft fairs, concerts, and outdoor festivals through the summer months. In fact, there is now more to do at Killington during the summer than there is during the ski season. By virtue of its close proximity to Killington, the Vermont Inn enjoys the same year-round traffic that has been attracted to the resort area.

Susan and Judd started in the inn business on August 1, 1988, when they purchased their inn. Ten years of successful Wall Street investment banking experience and an "empty nest" had driven the couple to seek a lifestyle change.

"We really enjoy being with people. We like sitting down with them in the living room and getting to know them better, and we get a kick out of receiving post cards from them from time to time between their visits here. It's enormously gratifying when a guest returns for repeat visits and essentially becomes part of the Ver-mont Inn 'family.' Since we have a rather sizable restaurant facility, we at times find the staffing and management of the restaurant somewhat overwhelming. Management of the restaurant and maintenance of our century-old physical plant are the facets of the business I like least.

"We live on the premises. We awaken at 7:30 and we're in the inn by 8:00. Our guests breakfast from 8 till 9:30 A.M. Susan will generally help out in the dining room while I work at the front desk assisting with check-out activities. Particularly in the sum-mer, we spend a lot of time helping the guests plan their various day trips and activities in the area. By 10:00 the inn is generally quiet again, and we try to spend a few minutes catching up on the paperwork of marketing, bills, and correspondence.

"At around 2:00 P.M. we return to our apartment for a nap. We try to squeeze in a short afternoon nap each afternoon. We've found it really recharges our batteries for the evening ahead.

We're back in the inn around 5:00, getting the inn ready for the evening activities. While we're napping, our staff handles the necessary housekeeping and takes care of the check-ins, so when we return for the evening most of the guest preliminaries have been handled.

"Susan and I generally serve as host and hostess in the dining room. We both try to get around to each of our guests to welcome them to our inn. We're in the dining room until 9:00 or 9:30 when the guests finish dinner and we adjourn to the living room for a conversation with our guests. We try to retire to our apartment by 10:00 or 10:30. Our staff closes the inn by about 11:00. During the winter the schedule might vary somewhat because we have to attend to the hot tub and sauna.

"We close the inn in April and May, and for a few weeks after the foliage season. Like our guests, we enjoy traveling. When we're not keeping the inn in the spring we often travel to Europe, and in the fall we try to get away to someplace warm like Hawaii, the Caribbean, or the desert in the southwestern U.S. We also enjoy staying at our own inn when we're closed. It takes on an entirely different feel, and it gives us a leisurely opportunity to spend the night in our own guest rooms. We've found it's the best way of getting a feel for our own facilities.

"From an advertising standpoint, we have found inn listings in the travel sections of newspapers like *The New York Times, The Boston Globe*, or *The New Jersey Star Ledger* to be quite effective. When people read the travel sections of their newspaper, they're already somewhat prequalifying themselves, so we find it to be money very well spent. We're a small inn, so we are not able to afford to buy even modest-size display advertising in the magazines to compete with the larger properties in our region. But when we find a 'listing' opportunity where we have the same thirty-word copy limitations as everyone else, then we do fine side by side with the major players.

"We've also found that highly focused direct mail works well for us. Our in-house inn newsletter serves as a very effective reminder to our former guests and the other people on our own mailing list.

"We are proud of a number of the successes we've enjoyed. This past year AAA upgraded us to a Three Diamond Inn, making us the only inn in Killington with that distinction. We've also been selected as the best restaurant in the Killington/Champlain fine dining category for the past three consecutive years. We're also proud of the dedication and longevity of our employees. Our head housekeeper has been here for a decade, and our head chef has been here for almost six years. Their professionalism and the stability of our overall staff have contributed immeasurably to the success of our endeavor.

"We do everything we can to ensure that our guests depart with a strong sense of the Vermont Inn being a place they want to come back to."

Part Three

OPERATING A COUNTRY INN

Louise Stewart, Pat Walter, and daughter, Bumpy, are joined by their staff on the steps of the Grant Corner Inn, Santa Fe. (Photo taken in 1987.)

TONY VINELLA

Chapter Twelve

YOUR STAFF AND YOUR GUEST

Staffing
Hiring Staff
Independent Contractors
Handling Employees

Serving Your Guest
The Inngoer's Bill of Rights
What's in a Name?

STAFFING

Innkeepers share one all-important challenge with every other small business owner in America: recruiting, training, and maintaining a staff of enthusiastic, knowledgeable, and dedicated employees. It is not unusual for aspiring innkeepers to assume that the least of their worries will be staffing the inn, when in fact the opposite is more often the case.

The working environment of a country inn is so close and so personal that the staff is like an extended family. And therein, very often, lies the heartache. A close working relationship means that the employees will mirror the dedication of the innkeepers, and that is as it should be. It also sets management up for disappointment when all does not go well with an employee.

"Without a doubt the area we found most difficult to grasp — and I'm not certain you ever master it fully — is personnel. Since we are perfectionists we have a tendency to expect the same dedication and commitment from our paid staff that we give the business ourselves. This kind of expectation can lead to some real frustration. When you have up to twenty-one employees at any given point in time, whether you're ready to admit it or not you are in the personnel business. It is very difficult to manage a staff of that size. It's not unlike being the mom and dad of twenty-one people. . . ."

A lot of innkeepers assume that once they "get over the crunch" of getting open and established, they'll be able to hire a few people and put their feet up a bit. Not so! One of the early lessons you will learn is that more staff does not equal fewer hours. In fact, added staff will almost certainly increase the amount of time you devote to your business. You'll be putting in the same or slightly more hours, but you'll find that the way you spend those hours will be dramatically different. In general, the management challenge shifts from physical to mental. Instead of hands-on, task-oriented activities, you will have to master the art of delegation.

Sorting through the various tasks of running a country inn, and clearly identifying those areas of the business most suited to your own talents and goals, will help you create the job descriptions for the missing players on your management team. Remember, running the inn is going to involve several different functions all working in tandem with each other. Here is an overview of the various operational components of a country inn.

Administration. The overall operational details of running the business include answering the telephone; booking and confirming reservations; preparing daily bank deposits; paying the bills; hiring, evaluating, and terminating employees; bookkeeping; opening and answering the mail; advertising; and promotion.

Maintenance. Daily, weekly, and monthly inspections and regularly scheduled maintenance of all equipment include heating, air conditioning, gutter cleaning, roof inspection and repair, drainage systems, refrigeration equipment, extermination, plumbing, painting, etc. Many of these functions can be performed on a part-time, handyman basis. Others, such as extermination, are better left to a professional service that performs regular inspections and applications under a blanket contract.

Housekeeping. Daily thorough cleaning of the guest rooms, baths, and common areas, laundering and replacing the linens, watering plants, freshening potpourri, replacing amenities and burned-out light bulbs, etc., all are the responsibility of housekeeping. Although every country innkeeper has probably made up every bed in his or her inn more than once, housekeeping is generally the category that is staffed from the opening day of the inn.

Hospitality. Meeting and greeting guests, check-in and check-out procedures, hosting tea and/or other meal functions, sharing hot chocolate or lemonade on the front porch, arranging flowers, etc., all make up the duties of the host and/or hostess of the inn. Clearly, this is the first role and responsibility of the innkeeper, and one most innkeepers have great difficulty assigning to others.

Food and Beverage ("F&B"). Kitchen operations must often produce and serve breakfast, tea, and dinner on a daily basis, as well as picnic baskets, midnight snacks, and whatever else the innkeeper has created as part of the inn's own unique food and beverage identity. Understandably, they are a complex and multi-faceted component of operating a successful country inn. The kitchen is a microcosm of the rest of the inn: within it are virtually all the tasks that must be handled throughout the establishment. In addition to the person who plans the menus, purchases the food, and prepares and presents the meals, there must be staff to serve the guests and clean up the kitchen after each meal period.

Often one member of the innkeeping management team will "specialize" in the kitchen side of the business. If neither member of the team has some solid prior experience in the fundamentals of running a restaurant, it would be a good idea to hire an experienced restaurateur to manage the kitchen side of the business. As Judd and Susan Levy quickly found out when they purchased the Vermont Inn in Killington, the day-to-day challenge of operating a full-service restaurant was a real eye-opener. *"We had done enough research on the inn business to have a reasonably good idea of what that was going to be like,"* explained Judd, *"but the restaurant end of the business turned out to be a business in and of itself."*

Hiring Staff

Staffing the "departments" of a successful country inn need not be a terribly daunting challenge, but because not all innkeepers have been employers in their past lives, it is important to keep a few fundamentals in mind. Let's assume you have decided that between the two of you, you'll handle the basic administrative and hospitality aspects of the inn. That leaves the maintenance, food and beverage, and housekeeping areas open for staffing assistance.

A word of caution. Since a big part of the charm of a country inn is its family atmosphere, hiring personnel with whom you feel a closeness is a good idea. But it is important that the "closeness" have its limits. As Louise Stewart of the Grant Corner Inn observed in her roundtable comments, the closeness of the staff can lead to a lot of heartache. When a staffperson lets you down by arriving late for work — or worse, not arriving at all — it is bad enough when it is simply a personnel issue. When you've embraced this employee as part of the family, it can be heartbreaking. Closeness is inevitable, but set up some ground rules going in and you'll save yourself considerable grief down the road.

Deal with each job applicant in a friendly, professional manner. Have a set application procedure in place to provide structure for each interview. Have all applicants — even the children of your best friend — fill out the same application. Standard employment application forms can be found at your neighborhood office supply store. Use one that avoids asking questions regarding age or marital status, or other potentially discriminating questions.

In addition, you might wish to have the applicant write a paragraph on why he or she is interested in working at your inn. This paragraph will tell you a lot about his or her grasp of basic written communications. Sentence structure and spelling may not seem terribly relevant to being able to make up the beds, but in a small operation, it's not a bad idea for the person who makes up the bed also to be able to take a reservation call if necessary.

One of the real pioneers in contemporary innkeeping, Signe Bergmann at the Preston House in Santa Fe, New Mexico, points with great pride to the fact that the lady who bakes for the inn has mastered virtually every other task on the premises as well. In fact, according to Signe, each person in the inn can do every other staffperson's job. Consequently, you get a sense of camaraderie among the Preston House staff that is truly unique.

When you interview prospective staff members, try to get a handle on how they might deal with the unexpected. Is the applicant easily rattled during the interview — or overly nervous? Does the applicant deal well with the interview? Remember, in this business one must deal with new situations and new people every day. Each staffperson will play a role in the all-important first impression the guest forms upon arriving at your inn.

The Law

When you become an employer, you graduate into a position that interests the government. Fortunately, since most country inns employ fewer than twenty-five people, many of the laws governing employer-employee relations do not apply to you. To be on the safe side, however, check with your lawyer, accountant, and/or the Department of Labor in Washington, D.C., to ensure that your business in in full compliance with current rules and regulations.

Termination

No matter how carefully you screen your applicants, there will be times when you must fire an employee. This is often perceived by country innkeepers as the toughest part of the job. It is important that one critical step be taken to protect yourself and your business from disgruntled former employees.

Make certain that substandard performance on the job is thoroughly documented and dated, and signed by the employee at the time the performance appraisal takes place. Repeated poor performance may be grounds for firing an employee, but be advised that even when a person is fired for incompetence, he or she is still eligible to collect unemployment compensation in many states.

Independent Contractors

Before you add an employee to your operation, make sure the tasks really require the addition of a full-time employee. Is it possible for someone else in your organization to perform these tasks? Could the tasks be performed by an independent contractor instead? Painting the exterior of the inn, maintaining the landscaping, even housekeeping services are all available through outside independent contractor services.

There are some distinct advantages to contracting with an independent contractor as opposed to hiring staff to perform certain duties in your operation. For example, when you use this type of service you can add or delete it as needed.

With an independent contractor you are not responsible for withholding tax, unemployment and disability insurance, or social security payments. You *are* responsible for filing a 1099 form with the IRS annually for each independent contractor to whom you paid more than $600.

The government carefully scrutinizes the status of independent contractors who might really be working as employees. The simplest test to determine whether a person is an employee or an independent contractor is *who sets the hours.* If you designate when the individual starts and stops work, then he or she is very likely an employee, and not an independent contractor.

Handling Employees

Once your staff is in place, be consistent in your standards and your insistence upon excellence. Cleanliness should be an absolutely non-negotiable item. You will establish other equally non-negotiable standards of operation before and after opening your country inn. A well-thought-out training program for new employees will save you a lot of headaches and heartaches down the road.

Spelling out, in writing, your standards of operation and such other items as attire, hair length, and demeanor is how an operations and training manual is created. As you gain experience, you will be able to develop a comprehensive manual of operating procedures and your mandated criteria for excellence.

However your manual is configured, it's a good idea to begin by stating the mission of your facility. In addition, an introduction to the innkeepers, their background, and the history of the inn are all excellent ways of preparing your new staff to deal with the questions your guests will be asking in the days, weeks, months, and (hopefully) years to come.

SERVING YOUR GUEST

Unfortunately, you'll not be setting your standards in a vacuum. Much of what a prospective employee brings to his or her first interview has nothing to do with you, your inn, or your standards. The work ethic, which a century ago was considered a fundamental part of the lives of Americans, has taken a severe beating in recent years. You'll be challenged by the bright young people who arrive at your door convinced that "waiting tables" or "making beds" is somehow beneath their station in life.

In America, service has grown to be considered something akin to indentured servitude. Children grow up thinking that service is the lowest form of money-making in existence. Young adults and students reluctantly accept jobs in the service sector when they can find no other acceptable alternative or simply to "hold them over" until they can find something better.

The next time you're in a restaurant, take a moment to initiate a conversation with your waiter or waitress. Chances are you'll meet a person who is on his or her way to doing something else. Our lack of respect for the service profession is surely a sad testimony to a set of community and personal values that have run aground.

By redefining service in the context of extending a gracious dining or lodging experience, you take the first step toward the European conception of the profession. In Europe, it is not considered demeaning for a man or woman to aspire to a career in the service industry. It is considered to be a worthwhile and respectable means of earning a good living.

Successful innkeepers consider serving others to be nothing short of a distinct honor and a privilege. As a result, they are on the leading edge of a contemporary redefinition of service in America. Those who have chosen to make this industry their life's work take a great deal of pride in serving their guest. Since you yourself are committed to service as a way of life, you will want and need to instill the same attitude in your employees.

The Inngoer's Bill of Rights

As an increasingly demanding public begins to set the minimum levels of acceptable country inn management, an inngoer's
bill of rights has been articulated by Sandra Soule, in her series
America's Wonderful Little Hotels and Inns.

- The right to personal safety
- The right to suitable cleanliness
- The right to comfortable, attractive rooms
- The right to a decent bathroom
- The right to privacy and discretion
- The right to good, healthful food
- The right to comfortable temperatures and noise levels
- The right to fair value
- The right to genuine hospitality
- The right to professionalism
- The right to a reasonable cancellation policy
- The right to efficient maintenance
- The right of people traveling alone to have all the above rights.

What's in a Name?

Every guest in your inn brings one fundamental characteristic to
your door: the desire to be served by name. Think about it for a
moment. In this increasingly mechanized society, nothing has quite the
melodic ring of hearing our own name used by those serving us.

Since most country inn visitors book their reservations in advance,
and provide certain details about themselves as part of making their
reservation, you have the advantage of being able to acknowledge this
person by name from the moment he or she arrives at your front door.
What's more, Mr. and Mrs. Guest should be introduced to the other
members of your staff who will be serving them, and should be referred
to by name at every encounter.

Once a guest is assigned to a guest room, you'll have fun identifying
all the places where you might find it possible to "personalize" his or
her visit at your inn. From the welcome note and fruit basket on the
desk in the room to the place card at the dinner table, your guest will
be flattered and you will be forever remembered as the inn that went a
little further to make him or her feel special.

Behind the Curtains . . .

The Carter House Inn, Eureka, California • Mark and Christie Carter.

One could consider the Carter House a constant "work in progress." At present the inn offers thirty guest rooms, and current growth plans call for another expansion to thirty-four guest rooms in the near future. Mark and Christie opened their inn years ago with three rooms, then expanded to seven, and then they bought the Hotel Carter, with twenty rooms, across the street. Bell House has three rooms nearby. Breakfast is served daily at the Hotel Carter, and dinner is served four nights per week.

The Carter House is a copy of an 1884 San Francisco Victorian mansion. The Carters originally began operation while still living in the mansion, to which they had moved from a small apartment. They had no furniture so they opened an art gallery and antique store on the premises, with inventory on consignment.

"We go out of our way to make the guest happy, and we pride ourselves on doing whatever it takes to please them. We believe that part of the responsibility of the innkeeper is familiarizing the guest with the local attractions. We serve wine and hors d'oeuvres early each evening between 5 and 6 P.M., which gives us a chance to introduce the guests to each other and give them the highlights of the area. We also put out tea and cookies later in the evening for our guests, which adds a lot to the homeyness of our inn. People come to our inn to relax, so we try to accommodate them by offering the amenities of a larger hotel, such as a valet service.

"Early every morning we offer fresh-baked pastries and tarts in a buffet presentation in the hotel and a full sit-down dining room breakfast in the Carter House. Between 7:30 and 10:00 we serve a full sit-down breakfast in the hotel.

"We've made arrangements with a number of the local tour operators to offer our vacationing guests a wide range of recreational and tour opportunities from river rafting to redwood tours. We also have a variety of golf courses in the area which our guests enjoy. Making the most of the local hospitality offerings is an important part of providing a well-rounded and multi-faceted experience for our guests. As a result of our close working relationship with the tour operators and restaurateurs in the area, we generate a significant number of guest referrals back from them to our inn.

"I think the inn business takes a lot of talent. You're dealing with people and with a physical plant. Both offer their own unique challenges. Just a month ago, we had a main water supply line burst and flood our dining room. Ten years ago we would have repaired it and hoped it would not happen again. Now we've learned that if one supply line is wearing out then they all are probably ready to become a problem, so we replaced all the lines to head off the next problem at the pass. But as surely as the sun rises there will be some other problem we've not anticipated — that's just the nature of the beast.

"As our inn keeps growing, our typical day-to-day duties keep changing. In the early years we might be cooking one minute and making up a guest room bed the next. As time has gone on and we've brought more people into the 'family' our duties have evolved into more administrative tasks like training, scheduling, and financial planning. Today, I take my children to school at 8:00 and get to the inn at about 8:15. I spend time with our guests and meet briefly with our staff each morning. After breakfast, I typically spend the mid-morning hours doing telephone work until check-out at 11:00. The mail comes at midday so we spend time responding to the mail and the myriad of details, from new guidebooks to donations.

"Three o'clock is check-in time and we try to be there to greet the guests on arrival to make certain their stay gets off on the right foot. Once they are checked in, we serve our wine and cheese at 5:00 until our dining room opens at 6:00 P.M. I try to stop by each table to make sure all is going well and that each guest is pleased.

"The main changes over the past decade include an industry-wide move to virtually all private baths. The amenities package in the rooms now includes VCR-equipped TVs, telephones in the bathroom, fireplaces, and a variety of special touches that reflect the increasingly demanding tastes of a discerning public. We aspire to be a five-star property, and our hospitality reflects those aspirations.

"We have found we need to promote more aggressively at some times of the year than others. During the winter months, for example, when fewer groups come through our area, we offer dinner-and-room promotional packages for our local clientele. It not only generates some volume at an otherwise slow time of the year, but it is also a terrific PR tool for reinforcing our presence in the community.

"We've also tried ideas that did not work. Several years ago we tried an expensive mailing to the residents of a community three hours away for a theater/dinner/overnight package. Out of 300 mailers we received no takers. When we analyzed why, we realized we had worked hard to sell the redwoods and other scenic wonders of our immediate area to people who also had redwoods and their own share of scenic wonders. Oh well, at least we've learned from our failures. As a result, our promotions have grown increasingly more effective each year.

"We always try to ask our guests how they found out about us. In this way we are able to have a much clearer focus in our marketing and advertising programs. With thirty guest rooms we serve approximately 1,000 people each month. We try to treat each one of these people as potential goodwill ambassadors for our inn — because that's exactly what they can be. When you're crossing paths with ten or twelve thousand people each year, you're generating eight to ten times that many potential word-of-mouth impressions."

Behind the Curtains . . .

The White Oak Inn, 60 miles N.E. of Columbus, Ohio • Joyce and Jim Acton.

The Actons' White Oak Inn has ten bedrooms, a dining room, and a common parlor/living area. This restored Ohio farmhouse was owned and operated by the Actons, who created the business, for seven years. On August 1, 1992, the Actons sold the inn. As Joyce explains it, the inn was not on the market, but someone came along with one of those proverbial "offers we simply could not refuse." At the time of the sale, the inn was performing well financially, and the owners were faced with a choice between expanding or selling at year's end.

"The most pleasant surprise we've had in this business has been the large number of very close friendships we've developed with people who originally visited us as guests of the inn.

"Without a doubt, the most difficult part of running the inn on a day-to-day basis was dealing with staff. Maintaining quality employees in a rural environment is a real challenge. Since many of our staff members were part-time, it was a constant battle to ensure they shared and exhibited our own dedication to high standards of service. In many ways the staffing of our business was also the most gratifying part of our experience. We touched the lives of a lot of young people and provided considerable opportunity for growth for many who have gone on to other responsible positions in the hospitality industry.

"In a small operation like ours, with ten guest rooms, you pretty much have to do everything. When you do have hired help it doesn't really diminish the amount of work you have to do, it just changes the nature of the work itself. You find if you're not actually turning over the guest room yourself you're busy making certain that someone else has done it correctly.

"A day in our inn begins at 5:30 A.M. and extends through breakfast at 7:30, check-out at 11:00, shopping, correspondence, administration, and errands until check-in at 3:00 P.M., followed by dinner at 6:00 P.M., socializing with guests until 10:00 or 10:30, and bedtime at 11:00.

"We really enjoyed the interaction with other innkeepers. We met a large number of open, caring, thoughtful people in the business who were extraordinarily generous with their good counsel and warm friendship. In fact, even though we've sold our inn, we plan to remain members of the Independent Innkeeper's Association just so we can maintain those contacts.

"I knew it would be busy, but I didn't expect it would be totally consuming. On the flip side of that, we were surprised by how pleasant the guest side of the business turned out to be. We made it a point to get to know each guest on a personal level, and that added a great dimension to our enjoyment of the business.

"When a guest leaves our inn, we want them to feel as though they have just left their `home away from home.' We've worked hard to create a relaxing casual environment with no hidden agenda, where they can do whatever they wish to do without fixed schedules. Our inn is a place where people can get away from their daily routines, their jobs, and the hectic mayhem of their weekday lives and sit in the porch swing, or sit by the fireplace and take a nap.

"We always try to give our guests some little memento or special experience during their visit. Whether it's our "Not So Very Famous Chocolate Chocolate Chip Chip Cookies," a cutting from our herb garden, or even a special piece of wood for a carving project, we try to make sure they leave with a unique recollection of their visit here."

The Hotel Carter (above) and its companion inn, the Carter House, in Eureka, California.

Chapter Thirteen

ADVERTISING AND PUBLIC RELATIONS

Brochures
Distributing Your Brochure

The Media
The Media/Inn Partnership
The Advertiser/Inn Partnership

Publicity and PR
Newsletters
Press Kits

Promoting Your Inn
Press Releases

Gift Certicates
Using Gift Certificates Creatively

Guidebooks

Webster's dictionary defines advertising as "the act of announcing by any of the techniques of advertising (i.e., radio, television, newspaper, magazine, direct mail, printed flyer, sandwich board) the availability of certain goods and/or services which are offered for sale." These goods or services might be offered to the general public or to a narrowly defined public. A member of that narrowly defined public who has been identified as a prime potential user of your goods or services is often referred to as your "target consumer."

What Webster's does not point out is that almost without exception, advertising costs money. I said "almost without exception" because there are in fact ways of acquiring paid advertising without actually having to pay cash. As an aspiring innkeeper, with your cash funds depleted by start-up costs, you would be well advised to master a wonderful technique called the "Trade-Out," or bartering.

Your ultimate success at bartering will depend upon a variety of factors outside your direct control, such as how much unsold inventory the media has that might be made available to you. You and the media have one thing very much in common — an inventory so perishable it is eliminated forever at the close of each day. Today's newspaper's unsold ad space, your unsold guest rooms, and the radio station's unsold commercials will not be here to sell tomorrow. As a result, it is in the best interests of all concerned to work toward a common promotional and marketing goal. As we discuss advertising we'll brainstorm about how these relationships might prosper. But first, let's look at several of the most common forms of advertising for innkeepers and how best you might use each of them.

BROCHURES

To begin, you'll find your money well spent on a simple brochure that provides the basic information a prospective guest might need prior to reserving a room. In preparation for creating your own, we recommend that you begin a collection of brochures, preferably most of them from inns you've personally visited. When you have about fifty of them you'll know the kinds of information innkeepers traditionally include in their promotional material.

In the interests of economy and utility, a simple two-fold 8 1/2" by 11" brochure, with one-third of one side designed to accommodate a gummed label or handwritten address, might be your best bet for a first-time brochure. Again, depending upon your budget, color photographs of the inn exterior, the common area, and at least one guest room will help your guest visualize your facility. Professional photographs will come in handy for other media as well, so either hire the best photographer you can afford or call up the local camera store and create a photo contest for their aspiring amateur customers.

Paper stock comes in hundreds of weights and finishes, and thousands of typestyle combinations are available to convey your ideas, so seek the advice of a professional. With quick copy printers all over the place, you'll have no difficulty acquiring a quick foundation in the basics of the business and a broad idea of the rates involved in producing your brochure.

Clean, forthright copy that conveys honestly what the inn is about and why a person might wish to visit works best of all. You'll find your guests will appreciate your candor. Remember, the Number One factor influencing the guest's opinion of an inn is the innkeeper. Personalizing your own brochure is a perfectly acceptable way of beginning a relationship with your prospective guest even before you have an opportunity to meet by telephone.

If color photographs of your inn are simply not possible for budgetary or time constraint reasons, then contact an art teacher and sponsor a pen-and-ink drawing contest. The best line drawing of your inn wins, and you incorporate that design into your own graphics. Or, with high-contrast black and white photography you can achieve the feel of a line drawing. If you need a "quickie" graphic, it is one approach you might like to explore.

Distributing Your Brochure

Once you have completed your brochure, the fun is just beginning. Getting your brochure into the hands of prospective guests becomes your next challenge. If you haven't already discovered it, mail is expensive! Make it your business to learn about the post office rate structure for classes of mail other than first class. Bulk rates, and grouping your outgoing mail by zip code, can save you substantial amounts of money if you are mailing in high quantities. If your quantities are low and your mailing is a highly focused and personalized one, then first-class postage is the way to go.

But mailing your brochure may end up being the least important channel of distribution available to you. Make it your business to locate all the local "take one" racks in town and see that your brochure is prominently displayed. You'll quickly realize how important this brochure is to you and your business. Make a game out of how many places you can identify as prospective circulation points for your brochure. The welcome centers located on interstate highways adjacent to state border lines are easy to identify, but you'll discover a broad array of other options. What about your favorite local florist or dry cleaner? Any retail operation not in direct competition with your inn is a potential drop point for your brochures — particularly if you do business with them personally!

THE MEDIA

The media you select to advertise your facility will be determined by your own research into your target customer, and by your budget. The challenge to advertising any retail business, and that includes inns, is how cost-effectively you can cross paths with your prospective guest. Once you have identified who your target is and where he or she lives and works, you will understand more clearly how best to reach them. If the out-of-town vacation traffic is important to your inn, for instance, access to and/or visibility on the nearest interstate highway might be a good idea. If most visitors to your community arrive by air, you'll want to explore how best you might get your message into the airport terminal.

Finding the appropriate media to reach your prospective guest is not as difficult as it might sound. Don't be afraid to shop around! Get to know the people who sell advertising for the local radio stations, television stations, newspapers, magazines, and outdoor sign companies. Whether you end up doing business with them or not, make it your business to remain current on their rates and information. The standard information package for the local newspaper and television station will generally contain a wealth of information on your market and your prospective customers.

The media folks are also terrific contacts for finding out what is going on in your own industry. Whether business is soft or trending upward, the people who make their living selling advertising in your community are among the first to know it. Once you have a complete "dossier" on all the prospective media in your area, you can formulate some general idea about which to purchase advertising from.

Advertising your business only brings a guest to your door the first time. Subsequent visits will depend upon how he or she enjoyed the first trip. If the experience at your inn was not a pleasant one, no amount of advertising will undo the negative impressions. Conversely, if the experience was a glowingly positive one, that satisfied guest will do more to generate other business for your inn than all the advertising you could purchase for years to come.

The combination of media you choose for your facility will probably include small, one-column ads in the travel sections of the daily newspapers that reach people seeking information on inns in your area. Pay attention to who is advertising what, everywhere in the marketplace. There is a lot to be learned from the patterns of advertising employed by other innkeepers.

Finally, you'll be pleasantly surprised how much you can learn by asking your colleagues. Successful innkeepers don't mind sharing ideas and information. As one of our roundtable members observed, when the inn down the road had a full parking lot they did too! Working together and sharing advertising "do's and don'ts" is a vital part of succeeding in this industry.

The Media/Inn Partnership

When you prepare to open your facility officially to the public, consider hosting a series of invitation-only "Soft Open Houses" with the various media serving as co-hosts. It is possible even to expand the function beyond the "open house" concept by perhaps featuring a "silent auction" or some other subtle fund-raising component to benefit one of the local community charities. There certainly is no shortage of need in every community, and with a little advance planning your inn can become the focal point for a broad range of media-centered, high-profile, worthwhile functions. It isn't necessary to go overboard on this idea. One or two ongoing functions to benefit the local art museum or the children's hospital will go a long way toward establishing you and your facility as responsible and involved members of the corporate community.

The relationship between a first-class country inn and the local media can take on the characteristics of a classic win-win arrangement. If you look upon the media as strictly providers of advertising time and space you are neglecting an important synergistic relationship that can contribute substantial revenues to your bottom line.

"With eight guest rooms we generate as much revenue as some eighteen- to twenty-room inns, for one very big reason: VISIBILITY! We've had full-page travel articles in important dailies like the Los Angeles Times *and widely read monthly publications like* Yankee magazine. Yankee *wrote a wonderful story about our Picnic Hamper concept. We created the Picnic Hamper idea more as a thematic hook for our inn than a money-making proposition, but to our surprise it's turned out to be nicely profitable.*

"When we started in the business in the early '80s, even though the industry was just beginning to blossom, travel editors all over the nation were writing about the cute little couple with the darling little Victorian inn. We spent a lot of time brainstorming about what we could do that would be original and copy worthy at the same time. Our Picnic Basket fit the bill perfectly."

The Advertiser/Inn Partnership

Every major purchaser of paid media is a potential promotional partner for your inn. In addition to the opportunities that await you in connection with the media, there are even more exciting possibilities among the media's customers. As we have already discussed, the comparatively few dollars available for purchasing advertising for a country inn require the innkeeper to be constantly aware of the unique cross-promotional opportunities that are constantly present and waiting to be exploited. Because of the lifestyle appeal of a country inn, cross-promotional concepts can touch a lot of consumer "hot buttons." For example, when a large upscale department store on the East Coast wanted to stimulate interest in its annual housewares sale, they launched a contest offering an all-expenses-paid inn weekend as the prize. The inns put up the prize in exchange for inclusion (with picture) in hundreds of thousands of the department store's advertising flyers. The department store added an appealing "entry" component to their sale, and the inns received more exposure through the newspaper supplements than they could have purchased with their entire annual budget.

Since car dealers, jewelry stores, florists, etc., all purchase media advertising on a regular basis, why not approach them and offer to "piggy-back" promotionally. Your inn can provide the romantic sizzle to make the local Chevrolet dealer's saleathon an appealing success.

Instead of simply decorating the Christmas tree, arrange for the local jeweler to decorate it with precious and semi-precious jewelry. Then you have a $100,000 Christmas tree — and a reason for people to visit your inn. When you reorient your thinking and creatively ponder the array of cross-promotional opportunities awaiting you, you'll be pleasantly surprised how many nice people you meet along the way. Your country inn is an important addition to the marketing and hospitality environment in your town.

PUBLICITY AND PR

Your ability to keep your inn in the public's eye will be a critically important component of your long-term success. Develop a media contact roster consisting of the news directors for all the broadcast media and the appropriate editorial contacts at the newspapers in your area. Don't overlook the smaller weekly newspapers. These publications are generally more interested in "softer" news items and will be more likely to publish your longer press releases in their entirety. Yes, I said press releases. It might take some getting used to, but your inn is going to be interesting to a lot of people, and part of the responsibility of the successful country innkeeper is a regular program of public communications.

Newsletters

At the heart of many such inn programs is a regular seasonal newsletter. Most newsletters are very simply produced in one color of ink and occasionally printed on colored stock. They are a great device for keeping your inn in your customer's mind. Since the newsletter targets inn guests, you'll have fewer in the early stages of operation and more later on.

As you go about visiting inns and accumulating their newsletters, you'll notice that these newsletters need not be terribly sophisticated documents. In fact, the more "folksy" and informal they are the better. I know that when I receive them it's something like getting a letter from an old friend — who reminds me I've been away too long!

Press Kits

Press kits are an important part of the increasingly professional world of contemporary country innkeeping. You need not have hundreds on hand at all times, but you'll find a well-thought-out press kit invaluable when the travel editor from the second largest daily newspaper in the Midwest calls to ask about this great little new inn he has heard so much about.

"Operationally, we found the time and effort we put into developing an open dialogue with newspaper travel editors to be worth its weight in gold. A well-thought-out press kit, to which these editors can refer, should contain all the pertinent facts and figures and historic tidbits about the inn. These travel editors are busy but their stock in trade is information, so if you take the time to include worthwhile information, it will get used. By regularly scheduling some special event at the inn such as open-hearth Thanksgiving, cooking school, herb lectures, etc., you give the travel editor a reason to mention your inn with some frequency. When these various articles and mentions appeared regularly, they had the effect of legitimizing our inn. This press attention was directly responsible for a considerable number of bookings."

As part of the research for this book, we have collected nearly 300 press kits of every imaginable size and description. Some even came with carefully packaged fresh-baked cookies enclosed! Press kits are for making a lasting impression on someone who might be in a position to stimulate interest in your inn. With that in mind, let's talk about what goes into a successful press kit — starting with that all-important first impression.

The recipient of your press kit will first encounter the envelope in which you've placed your press kit. The U.S. Postal Service will provide you with an unlimited quantity of sturdy two-pound capacity cardboard PRIORITY envelopes free of charge. These envelopes (and their contents) get immediate attention because they so closely resemble the much more expensive EXPRESS mail and FEDEX packages. But they cost only $2.90 to send anywhere in the U.S. for delivery within two days. Not a bad deal.

To differentiate your priority mail from another inn's priority mail, you can stamp a message such as: confidential, priority, urgent, etc. These are available at your local office-supply store, or you can order your own in any color ink, with the name of your inn incorporated into the stamp. Some inns affix metallic gummed stickers touting their most recent Uncle Ben's Inn of the Year standing or their newest Mobil or

AAA ratings on their outgoing mail and priority packages.

Press Kit Checklist
Within an aesthetically pleasing pocket folder or three-ring binder include:
- A statement of your inn's history
- Your inn brochure, including: an inset map to your inn; hours of operation; telephone and fax numbers; reservation, children, pet, and smoking policies; description of guest rooms; range of rates
- Recent articles featuring your inn
- Menus
- Innkeeper profiles
- Photo business card
- Special features and services, e.g., hiking trails, wine tastings, canoe trips, cooking classes, picnic baskets.
- Supplementary promotional material — targeted for specific types of customer

A Sample Press Kit
The press kit of the Asa Ransom House in Clarence, New York, stands out for several reasons. First, Robert and Judy Lenz have cleverly made use of a simple coated white stock pocket folder with no printing. The folder says "clean and fresh" without uttering a printed word. The Lenzes customize this simple white folder by affixing the gummed seal of their inn to the upper right corner. Their seal is elegantly printed in green on white stock, with the name of the inn, a line drawing of the inn, and the line: "Fine Country Dining, Lodging, & Gifts. Clarence, New York." The innkeepers have further customized their label by carefully hand lettering, in matching green ink, "Press Kit '93." On the lower left corner of the folder they have affixed the seal of the Independent Innkeepers Association to which they belong. The entire pocket folder is tied up with a narrow white and green ribbon that has Asa Ransom House printed in a repeating pattern along its entire length.

Your press kit may contain whatever you wish to share with your recipient, from hand-written personal notes to recipes, but it should also contain a few basics. Bear in mind that you are providing this information as a comprehensive overview of what goes on at your inn. The recipient should be able to write an accurate description of your facility based on the materials you've included. In addition, if the press kit has done its job, the recipient will almost certainly be compelled to pay a visit at the next convenient opportunity.

With the Asa Ransom press kit, the first impression of the materials in the folder is one of consistency. Every printed piece uses that same Asa Ransom green ink on buff or cream stock. Although the stock color remains the same for the menus, they are printed in a dark brown ink, which I am confident is more readable in the evening light of the dining room. The Asa Ransom press kit begins with a clearly typed cover letter presented on the inn's letterhead. Once again, the inn logo appears in a combination of green and brown inks on the same cream-colored stock.

In addition to the cover letter and the menu, the inn has included:

- An accommodation summary describing each guest room's sleeping configuration (king, queen, double, or canopy beds), special features (i.e., fireplace, parlor, balcony or porch), and price levels (depending upon meals included).
- Two color postcards showing two separate guest rooms.
- A one-page flyer promoting the inn's winter getaway package and special gourmet nights.
- Five sleeved 35mm color slides of the inn, suitable for reproduction.
- A one-page reprint of the local newspaper review of the inn.
- Actual tear sheets from *Country Living* magazine depicting the inn in color.
- An "Invitation to Tea" one-fold flyer cross-promoting the gift certificates on the back panel.
- An Asa Ransom House background piece produced like a personalized newsletter presenting the history of the inn, its professional associations, guest rooms, public spaces, dining facilities, and nearby sight-seeing opportunities, and featuring an inset road map with precise directions to the inn. This piece has an address space on one panel so it can perform as a comparatively low-cost information piece for those inquiring about the inn.

This well-prepared and -presented press kit might be even more beneficial to a reviewer if it contained thumbnail bios on the innkeepers themselves. If innkeeper pictures are included, and they are a superb addition, they should be taken somewhere inside or directly in front of the inn itself. Playing up the personal involvement of the innkeeper will further differentiate this inn from all other lodging facilities.

PROMOTING YOUR INN

With your brochure in hand and your shiny new press kit ready to be sent at the drop of a hat, let's examine how you might put these tools to work in publicizing and promoting your inn. Your local public relations effort actually begins long before you open the door for business. Most successful keepers of country inns are actively involved in their local chambers of commerce and other similar business development organizations. Even if you've never been a joiner in your life, start now. Plan to become not just a *member* but a *player.*

Make it your business to contribute your time and your ideas to the local business community. Even before the inn opens, when you make the deal to acquire the inn, or the building you plan to convert to that use, or the land upon which you plan to erect your inn, tell the public about it. Distribute a well-thought-out press release that announces your intentions and contains a current picture of you and your partner or family, as well as a clean stat of your logo and anything else that might help the public better understand your plans. Once you have drawings and plans of your new inn, get out in the community and share them.

People enjoy watching a work in progress. Let the local civic clubs know you're available to bring along "before and after" slides of your work in progress and present them as one of their midday lunch programs. You'll be pleasantly surprised by how many invitations you receive once people know you are willing to come and talk about your inn. Each time you make a presentation or schedule one, send out a press release announcing those plans.

Be on the lookout for local opportunities to shine. If the community knows you are available for garden club tours, historic society brunches, or ladies' auxiliary teas, and that you are eager to make them all feel welcome, they will come.

"We've combined our love for cooking with otherwise slow times between seasons into an important business opportunity for the inn. We conduct a two- or three-day cooking school several times each year, with excellent results. We've been able to attract people from both coasts to Vermont for a challenging and fun weekend of food, fun, and learning. The success of our cooking school is a great reinforcement for the restaurant side of the business, and our Mobil 4 Star rating helps our cooking school. It all works very nicely, one in

concert with the other.

"There are a surprising number of potential revenue sources that the uninitiated innkeeper sometimes overlooks. Assuming some modest success in the business, there are money-making opportunities in such areas as specialty picnic lunches, theme dinners and/or brunches, moderately upscale wines to accompany dinner, consulting and speaking engagements, cooking schools, inn-specific special merchandise and gifts, paid inn endorsements for manufactured products, original books, consignment sale of the work of local artists, etc., etc."

Press Releases

Any unique concepts that originate at your inn, from revenue-enhancing cooking schools to gourmet picnic baskets, are newsworthy and will be treated as such by the trade press — if you handle the information in a professional manner.

- Try to keep all your press releases to one page.
- Use a consistent layout that can be easily understood by the recipient.
- State at the top of the press release when it may be used. "For Immediate Release" is appropriate.
- Note your name, address, and telephone number as the contact "For Additional Information."
- Have a succinct one-line lead as heading. For example: "Raintree Inn Receives National Award."
- The one-page release should have the standard who-what-where-when-why basics.
- End with three asterisks centered at the bottom of the page to signify that that is all the material contained in this particular release.

GIFT CERTIFICATES

Gift certificates are generally used in two ways. They are sold by the inn to persons wishing to give them as gifts to others, and/or they are issued by the innkeeper as a promotional or goodwill gesture, aimed at stimulating additional inn business. They can be an important revenue generator and a flexible merchandising tool, but there are some rules to using them. And the more effort you put into making the gift certificate look and feel special — and valuable — the more successful you'll be in marketing it.

In addition to your logo and whatever special design you come up with, never issue a gift certificate that is redeemable at your inn without the ground rules being printed on it. Even when it has been purchased as a gift, it is important that an expiration date be entered on the certificate and enforced. Generally when a gift certificate is purchased, an expiration date of one year from the date of issue is appropriate. On gift certificates issued for promotional purposes, you might wish to restrict the redemption period to just six months.

You may also add other redemption criteria. For example, the bearer of the gift certificate may only redeem it Monday through Thursday evenings — or perhaps the certificate is redeemable for lodging and food only, and not for alcoholic beverages or gifts. Since you have created the promotional opportunity, it will be up to you to define the redemption ground rules. Almost without exception, these ground rules will be accepted without question, since the recipient has received it for free.

Always enter the maximum redemption value of the gift certificate in U.S. dollars, and clearly articulate that the certificate is redeemable for lodging, food, and gifts only, and not for cash. Otherwise, you run the risk of having gift certificates show up with the redeemer demanding cash for the unused face value of the certificate. Don't laugh. It happens. The next time you pick up a gift certificate or a discount coupon for a consumer product pay attention to the actual cash value printed somewhere on the certificate — usually it is 1/10 of one cent. Now you know why.

Two last administrative suggestions: all gift certificates, whether issued promotionally or sold in the inn, should have an authorization signature affixed at the time they are issued. Finally, gift certificates should be treated as if they were money. It is important that they be inventoried, sequentially numbered, and stored in the safe or cash register with the other cash money. Maintain the same controls that you establish for handling cash, and teach your staff to do the same.

Using Gift Certificates Creatively

Plan to make gift certificates a vital operating component of your inn and you'll be pleasantly surprised by how many you sell. The sale of gift certificates, however, is only one way you can incorporate this program into your operation.

Reciprocal trade agreements are a superb way to combine the best interests of the inn and the media. Gift certificates can become the means of accomplishing your promotional goals as well. For example, distribute a few to the key decision-makers in your community who perhaps have not yet visited your inn.

Since the media, especially the radio and television stations serving your market, want to generate excitement among their viewers and listeners, they can help you create an inn-centered promotional opportunity that is exciting, fresh, and new. Assume for a moment that you would like to increase the amount of "special occasion" celebration business at your inn. And let's assume you'd like to work out a cross-promotion with the classical music radio station in the town 25 miles north of the inn. You could sponsor a contest, offering as prize not just one all-expenses-paid anniversary weekend at your inn — but the same number of weekends as the couple is celebrating in years. If it's the lucky couple's seventh anniversary, the prize is seven anniversary weekends at your inn. This could be a simple postcard entry random drawing, or it could be a 100-words-or-less written entry describing why that particular couple deserves to win. The entries become additional names for your inn's mailing list — and the radio station ends up with a dynamite promotional concept that you agree to do exclusively with them every year.

Here's a different twist on selling gift certificates. Sit down with the local Cystic Fibrosis Foundation or Children's Hospital and offer to donate some portion of all gift certificate sales for the next year to their organization. They then become your ambassadors of goodwill — and prime potential purchasers of your gift certificates at the same time. P.S. It's also a very nice thing to do for others.

> Any promotion or barter you create as a country inn should be tailored to stimulate volume in a highly focused segment of the business. The more time and effort you spend identifying and clearly articulating the goals for your particular promotion, the more likely it will be that the promotion will match your need — and the results, exactly what you seek.

GUIDEBOOKS

Other than time-honored word-of-mouth advertising, the Number One resource used by your prospective guest will be one or more guidebooks. Like every other aspect of this rapidly growing industry, there are highly focused guidebooks on everything from where to stay if you simply must travel with your beloved basset hound to vegetarian hot spots to non-smoking inns, family inns, and inns that cater to the gourmet palate.

The Professional Association of Innkeepers International publishes a $25 *Guide to the Inn Guidebooks*, which is a superb reference tool for innkeepers. In their fifth edition they have researched and listed approximately 200 different inn guidebooks, most of them available to the innkeeper free of charge. The PAII guide includes helpful information on such things as publication deadlines, fax numbers, size of the print run, and the authors' criteria for selecting inns for inclusion. This is one $25 dollar investment you'll be glad you made!

Perhaps surprisingly, more than 80 percent of the guidebooks listed do not charge for listing inns. PAII keeps the *Guide to the Inn Guidebooks* updated as part of its member services. For complete details, call 1-805-569-1853, or FAX: 805-682-1016.

> PAII offers several hints for getting your inn listed in guidebooks, including:
> - Grab the guidebook author's attention by focusing on his or her area of expertise. For example, if the author specializes in architecture, focus your information on your inn's architectural history.
> - Always send along the best photograph you can afford, along with a personal note to the author outlining the highlights of the inn.

> *Behind the Curtains . . .*
>
> **The Grant Corner Inn**, Santa Fe, New Mexico • Lousie Stewart and Pat Walters.
>
> Here you'll meet the husband and wife team with two last names, and one delightful young daughter named Bumpy. Louise Stewart and Pat Walters, innkeepers, serve a full breakfast daily, and Pat's weekend gourmet brunches are rapidly becoming a Santa Fe tradition.
>
> "The thing about Santa Fe is the vast number of cultures represented here. It has always been very important to us to be part of this community. Everything we can do to interact with and be part of the community finds its way back to us. They are your

bread and butter and they deserve to be treated as such. They support you, they promote you, they can destroy you, or they can help you to grow.

"We've often discussed what would happen if for some reason Santa Fe was no longer the tourist mecca it is today. We would need a combination of endless promotional creativity and very deep pockets. Many people in the innkeeping business are faced every day with precisely that challenge. They fell in love with a building, or a quaint and lovely little town, and they now must deal with the cold hard reality of stimulating business in order to survive. We're very spoiled here in Santa Fe.

"Santa Fe has a deep-rooted appeal in its variety of cultures and its unusual architecture and history. As a historic trading crossroads this community has proven its staying power over time. Oh sure, we expect that the 'Coyote Bandanna' trend currently sweeping the country will run its course. But the rich recreational and artistic heritage of this community will prevail.

"Our guests are a real pleasure. They are usually on vacation and their attitude is relaxed and generally very easy-going. But we take our guests' comments very seriously. When they point out a burned-out bulb we act on it immediately. The savvy innkeeper will do one thing periodically — STAY IN YOUR OWN GUEST ROOMS. Putting your own personal imprint on your inn should not be accomplished at the expense of the guest's comfort. We've found that the longer you are in this business, the better you get at striking that comfortable compromise between unique and utilitarian. Whatever you do it has to be practical and durable.

"The way we've learned these lessons is by listening to our guests. You must constantly solicit their input, whether with a simple comment card or face to face. Over the years it is amazing how many thoughtful guest comments have resulted in our changing the way we do business.

"After several guests suggested them, for example, we put full-length mirrors in all our rooms. Night stands on both sides of the bed, where guests can place book, reading glasses, and water, have become a standard part of our guest room decor. In the bath area we added a countertop with sufficient space for the guest's personal toiletries, hair driers, etc. Since we have so many repeat guests, they've gotten to the point where they'll pull us aside and request special additions to their favorite room for their next visit.

"I arrived at the inn this morning at 8:00 and served as the hostess for our brunch. Afterward we had an employee meeting to discuss our plans for the holidays and how we were going to handle our Thanksgiving and Christmas dinners. We also covered our charity bazaar which this year will benefit the homeless. Later we met with the kitchen staff to review menus for the holidays and to plan a 'dry run' of the menus to try out this year's recipes. The holidays are very special for us so we always try to outdo ourselves.

"In the afternoon we take care of maintenance like leaky faucets. The inn business can give you a lot of crazy days. Christmas two years ago, several of our staff failed to show up for work, so Pat, Bumpy, and I spent fifteen hours at the inn doing everything from cooking food to cleaning guest rooms. It's just part of the business.

"The nicest comment we hear on a regular basis is 'You have such a flair for detail.' People notice the little things we do, and they appreciate that it's the little touches that separate us from the larger hotels and chain operations. The other compliment we love to hear is how friendly our staff is and how amazing they are with recalling names.

"We heavily emphasize word-of-mouth advertising, but we do participate minimally in the New Mexico B&B advertising program. Another very effective advertising tool for us has been our breakfast. We invite the public to join our guests for breakfast on a space-available basis, and it has really paid off for us. We estimate that 25 to 30 percent of our bookings are a direct result of someone who has visited us for breakfast and followed up by suggesting or making a reservation to stay with us."

Tom and Margaret Ray, owners, at the Oaks, Christiansburg, Virginia. The inn is decorated for Christmas in high Victorian style.

Chapter Fourteen

OPERATING POLICIES AND PROCEDURES

TELEPHONES

We've often mentioned the importance of first impressions. Many of your guests' first impressions of you and your inn will be by telephone. Entire workshops have been created around the creative use of the telephone, perhaps the most indispensable tool in the innkeeper's bag of tricks. Here are a few thoughts about the telephone and its role in your business.

First of all, and at the risk of sounding redundant, be consistent. Figure out the greeting you want to have delivered and write it down for all to memorize. For example: "Greetings from the White Willow Inn, how may we serve you?" If that's your standardized greeting, make certain all the employees who are permitted to answer the telephone know it. It's also a good idea to make sure who in the organization is primarily responsible for the telephone, and to give that person the latitude to get the job done. That means once they've been made to understand the role of the telephone, it is their responsibility to see that it gets answered properly.

Every staffmember should be made to appreciate a ringing phone. When they understand that the more it rings, the more the inn will be serving guests — and that's what keeps people in innkeeping employed — then they are more likely to treat each telephone call like a reservation. In fact, each prospective guest call is either a reservation now or a reservation later, so each should be handled by a courteous and friendly person on the inn's end of the line.

Soon you will be anticipating most of the questions asked by prospective guests. Until then, however, it might be a good idea to post the answers to the most often asked questions in your employee manual and on the bulletin board for all to see. Generally, a clear, easy-to-understand list of rates should lead the list of operation information. Next, availability (as determined by the reservation book), brochure requests, and such details as directions on locating the inn and check-in and check-out times should be memorized by anyone authorized to answer your telephone.

If your inn is located in an out-of-the-way place, pre-write the directions to your property as simply and directly as possible starting from callers' likely points of origin. For example, if the bulk of your business will be coming from the next largest town due west of your inn, identify the primary arteries and develop your directions from a point your caller will recognize. Carefully drawn and printed maps provide additional visual aids in helping people find their way to your doorstep. (See page 166–167 for suggestions on creating brochures.)

Do not be dismayed by the "shoppers" who seem to make a hobby out of comparing rates and data on inns in your area. Think of the two or three minutes you have with them on the telephone as your opportunity to showcase what makes your inn different, while enjoying their undivided attention. Be helpful. Your knowledge of the area and its attractions is an important asset.

Prospective guests appreciate it when the innkeeper is able to make side-trip suggestions and speak knowledgeably about highway conditions and distances between certain stops. It is human nature to wish to cut off a rambling inquirer when your fresh-baked bread is coming out of the oven, the other line is ringing, and two early arrivals are entering through the front door. Try to resist the temptation. Each caller deserves your undivided attention. Eventually you'll master the technique of that swan mentioned earlier — gently seeming to traverse a placid summer pond as you paddle like a poodle just beneath the surface.

Answering Machines

If you are alone in the inn, completely "snowed under" and unable to give the caller the attention he or she deserves, then the answering machine can be a last resort. But use it sparingly — and creatively.

It is quite possible to prepare an outgoing message that conveys warmth, humor, hospitality, and professionalism, without being nauseatingly cute. Although you'll want to record your own and individualize it to your heart's content, here is an approach that might get your creative juices flowing:

". . . Hello and thank you very much for calling the Raintree Inn. I'm Sally, one of the innkeepers, and I'm up to my elbows in apple pie crust, so please take a moment and leave your name and number at the tone. Your call is very important to us — as you'll be able tell by how quickly we return it!"

If this particular type of personalized call works for you, that's great. But be aware that the more individualized and unique the message is, the more quickly it will be recalled — particularly if a prospective guest has the frustration of hearing your "apple pie crust" line six times in a row. The idea here is simply to vary your message — but keep it unique, comfortable, and individualized to match your inn.

Toll-Free Numbers

In all likelihood a substantial portion of your business will be out-of-town visitors to the area. With computerized long distance telephone services now more competitive than ever before, there is no excuse not to have your own incoming toll-free telephone number. A small business need not invest huge sums of money today in order to handle itself the same way a large business does in the eyes of the consumer.

Your toll-free number need not incorporate the name of your inn, as does the Rabbit Hill Inn's 1-800-76-BUNNY or the Governor's Inn's 1-800 GOVERNOR. (Incidentally, as you may note, that last number has one too many digits. The last digit makes no difference in the destination of the call, so the Marbles just added the last "r" or 7 in order to complete the word.)

There are lots of interesting and creative ways to make your number more memorable. The point is that toll-free numbers work and they are now affordable for a small business.

RESERVATIONS

Most successful country inn keepers have a clearly articulated booking policy that is provided to each guest at the time the reservation is made. Don't forget that a warm, hospitable, and personable country inn is also a business. If you fail to set and enforce a non-refundable deposit policy it will cost you money and business in the long haul. That said, you can make the judgment call that best suits your and your guest's needs, whenever necessary. Your policies will be best understood as guidelines for yourself and your staff, not as cast in stone.

If your inn is located in a high-traffic destination location, such as Santa Fe or Savannah, or in an area with a clearly defined "high" season, such as the ski season in Vermont, it will help if you establish firm policies for when you will accept and confirm a reservation and when you will not. Generally, a room will be held for an arriving guest who has prepaid for all or part of his or her lodging. The amount of deposit will vary depending upon the inn, from one night's lodging to hold a guest room for one or two evenings, to a larger deposit for multiple nights.

You may also find it helpful to state clearly in your reservation policies that when the deposit is accepted for multiple nights, it is applied to the last night first. In this way the guest understands that shortening the stay mid-visit will cost a minimum of one night's lodging cost. You need only hold an empty room without a deposit once, while declining other revenue-generating business, to understand how and why a reservation policy is necessary.

RECORD KEEPING

The Message Book

There are two critically important record-keeping tools that should have a permanent home near the telephone most often used for inn business. First, a spiral-bound message book with carbonless second-copy sheets should be handy and USED for all incoming messages. Even if it's just the two of you at first, you will find this system of documenting messages invaluable. The carbonless copy pages remain in the book, once the message itself has been removed, and you have a permanent, easily accessible record of calls, dates, numbers, and subjects. These books even have a place on the front panel for noting the inclusive dates of the messages contained in each book. As you fill one you can simply file it behind the last one on the shelf and access it as needed. Over time you will develop your own best system for keeping track of frequent guests, primary vendors, tradesmen, etc., but in the interim, your message book can serve as a handy tool.

The Reservation Form

The second tool is the most important record in your business — your reservation form. It can be as simple or as fancy as you wish. A simple layout in a three-ring loose-leaf binder might be an ideal beginning system. Later, as your procedures grow more refined and your systems become more structurally established, you might consider investing in custom-designed carbonless copy reservation forms which permit you to write a guest confirmation at the same time you are entering the reservation information. And at some point you will find yourself computerizing the entire reservation form and process. Easier-to-use software and dramatically more user-friendly hardware will make it a pleasure to incorporate the computer into all aspects of administering your country inn.

Regardless of the system you elect to use, each reservation form will need certain basic fundamental information, including:

- Name, address, and telephone number of person making the reservation
- Day(s) and date(s) requested by guest
- Number in party
- Preferred payment method — credit card type, account number, and expiration date
- Deposit amount requested? Date deposit received?

In addition, certain supplementary information will become extremely important to the profitability of your country inn, as your business matures and prospers. For example:

- **Source.** Where did you hear about us? NOTE: If the guest has been referred by a former guest or friend of the inn (and there will be many), try to get the person's name in order to send them a thank you note.
- **Policies.** It is a good idea to recap the policies of the inn relative to smoking, pets, children, check-in times, check-out times, etc., at the time the reservation is made. In order to make certain these topics are covered with the guest, a "Policies Conveyed" check box will serve as a handy reminder. Once the policy items have been discussed, and the box checked, you have a permanent record for your files and for your future reference.
- **Individual Needs of Guest.** Having first-hand knowledge of a special anniversary or birthday celebration is another way to personalize the guest's stay at your inn. And determining now whether any member of your guest's party is physically challenged and requires a wheelchair-accessible entrance, guest room, and bath will permit you to allocate your rooms accordingly. The individualized attention to detail you are able to provide will differentiate you and your facility from every other lodging experience the guest has had in the past.
- **Directions.** Determine whether the guest is planning to arrive by automobile or air so you can include specific location instructions in the confirmation.

Confirming The Reservation

If the guest is confirming his or her reservation and guaranteeing it by credit card, your confirmation should be mailed immediately upon securing credit authorization on the card equal to the agreed-upon amount of the deposit. If payment of the deposit is going to be made by check, the confirmation should be held until the check arrives and sent immediately to the guest at that time.

The confirmation is your first opportunity to initiate contact with the guest in a manner completely of your own choosing. Use it well. The reservation conservation package should include your brochure, directions to the inn, a restatement of your policies, and a well-thought-out and carefully composed confirmation letter restating the agreed-upon reservation terms and deposit arrangements.

Cancellation Policies

In your inn policies it is important that you spell out very clearly what happens in the event of a cancellation. For example, you might have a full deposit refund policy if the cancellation is received fourteen days prior to arrival, or you might choose to have a fixed cancellation processing fee of $15 no matter how much advance notice you're given. Matters of finance and rigid refund policies are completely up to you as the innkeeper, but some plan for handling the flow of funds in an equitable manner will save you considerable grief when you are faced with a last-minute cancellation.

One way to deal with last-minute cancellations is to explain that you will endeavor to resell the guest room and if you are successful, the deposit will be refunded. In the event the room goes unsold, the guest forfeits some or all of the deposit. In the spirit of making lemonade out of lemons, an offer to apply some or all of the deposit to a future visit might also make sense as you assemble the day-to-day policies of your inn.

As we spoke with innkeepers on the topic of setting and maintaining refund policies, their perceptions varied a great deal with the number of years they had been successfully involved in the business.

"When we first opened we were not strict about collecting for cancellations and it resulted in a lot of lost revenue for rooms which we held and never filled after a last-minute cancellation. Now we are very specific about our ten-day cancellation policy, and we do not accept a reservation without a valid and verified credit card. Pre-

sented properly and from the outset, the guest understands the ground rules and you avoid the possibility of embarrassment and confusion at a later date."

"They say as you get older you grow more rigid in your approach to life. I guess we're either not getting older or this business has mellowed us over the last decade. As a case in point, we've evolved a more flexible approach to cancellations during our slower seasons. If we receive a cancellation at a time when we were not booked full and turning guests away, we're less inclined to bill the guest for the full price of the room today than we might have been in the early days."

From this same innkeeper we learned that flexibility can indeed have its limits, particularly in the "high season" when an empty guest room is money lost forever. *"If we're in the middle of our foliage or heavily booked ski season and someone cancels at the last minute, we will adhere firmly to our cancellation policy."*

CHILDREN, PETS, AND SMOKING

Before you fold your arms and dismiss these three management challenges with a flip "none of the above," carefully consider what downside impact each prohibition might have on your operation. Whether you care to admit it, prohibiting any one of these items in your inn is going to cost you some business. Alas, like life, innkeeping is chock-full of trade-offs.

Children

As you travel around the country visiting inns, you will no doubt observe that inns that are frequented by couples with children in tow are very few and far between. There is good reason for this. Country inns generally do not offer activities or facilities that appeal to young children. Prior to setting your own policies relative to serving children in your inn, it is a good idea to do two things. First, give careful consideration to the marketing statement you have written for your property (see page 87). Ideally, within that statement you have defined your target customer. That customer should be given primary consideration as you ponder your policies on children. Certainly, such items as fragile antiques and *objets d'art* should also be given thought, but ultimately, your target customer is your first and foremost consideration.

Bear in mind that your policies regarding children will be read by potential guests who seek the solace of a country inn specifically to avoid small children. The antithesis is also true. Those families with small children seeking a vacation that they can all enjoy together are quickly drawn to the inn that caters to their needs — and promotes itself accordingly.

> Before instituting a final policy on children, take a moment to research your inn guidebooks and determine the policies of other successful innkeepers. As you will quickly observe, very few innkeepers specifically prohibit children. They have, however, created a variety of ways to articulate their policies.
> "Children over 12 accepted"
> "Children over 12 OK in carriage house"
> "Appropriate for children over 12"
> "School-age children OK"
> "Inquire regarding children"
> "Older children welcome"

Pets

Unlike the somewhat touchy dilemma of policies regarding children, the issue of pets is considerably less emotional, with the rare exception.

If you are in a municipality that has no health department regulations specifically prohibiting pets on the premises, you will need to make some judgment calls on this. Here once again, it is a good idea to review how other successful innkeepers have established their own policies. Country inns that welcome pets are even rarer than inns that welcome children.

If guests insist on bringing their pet along, you can generally appease them by suggesting that they keep their "baby" in a portable pet kennel with them in their rooms. If the pet is too large or the guest is simply unwilling to comply, many innkeepers solve the problem by making special overnight kennel arrangements with the nearest vet.

Smoking

In a nation where the smoking population is shrinking each year, it is a challenge to devise a policy that is fair to all your guests, including those who choose to smoke. Precisely because of the strong emotions that surround this issue, those who continue to smoke are often a very determined and vocal minority of the population and many of them would like very much to visit your inn.

> The wide variety of published innkeeper policies relative to smoking is clear evidence of the sensitivity of this issue within the industry.
> "Smoking permitted only in common area rooms"
> "Smoking in restricted areas"
> "Limited smoking"
> "Smoking allowed in bar"
> "Smoking permitted on porches only"
> "Non-smoking dining room"
> "Smoking restricted"
> "Smoking not encouraged"
> "Some smoking rooms available"

Due to the volatility of the smoking debate, it is important that your policies be clearly stated for all to see. The absence of ashtrays and matches may be clear evidence of your wishes but cannot be relied on exclusively to communicate your policies.

CHECK-IN AND CHECK-OUT TIMES

In order to establish your inn's check-in and -out times, it's a good idea to begin by setting the earliest and latest time a guest may check into the inn each day. This time period is considerably more important to you as the innkeeper of a small intimate facility than it is to a large convention-style hotel, because greeting your guest personally is often one of the most enjoyable parts of the job of running a country inn. Keep in mind that the Number One reason people return to a particular inn — and what they remember most about their experience — is the innkeeper. Therefore you'll not want to miss that one opportunity to make a good first impression.

Generally, a check-in time period of three hours in the afternoon will permit you to receive most of your arriving guests personally. Often the 4:00 to 7:00 P.M. period will permit you to greet arriving guests and mingle with those who have chosen to take afternoon tea as well. Some flexibility is necessary with this policy as with all others, but clearly stating it on your confirmation materials will help you manage the business rather than it managing you.

Check-out times can be extrapolated backwards from the 4:00 P.M. check-in period. Depending on the size of your inn and your house-keeping staff, you can compute how long it will take to prepare the inn for the evening's arriving guests. As a matter of course, most innkeep-ers say goodbye to their guests after breakfast, and check-out actually occurs between 8:30 and 10:00 A.M. These times may vary depending upon your area, but it is a good idea not to leave the check-out time to chance. It is always possible to vary the policy as needed.

TIPPING

Tips for housekeepers and/or kitchen service personnel are one of the most regionalized issues in the country inn business. Larger resort hotel properties often make it clear that a flat service charge will be added to all bills and distributed to all appropriate personnel. Still other successful members of the hospitality industry go so far as to place "tip envelopes" in the guest room, as is done on some cruise ships.

In general, if tipping is going to be made an automatic part of the service process anywhere in your country inn, it would be most permis-sible and least obtrusive in the dining room. If you add an automatic gratuity of 12 to 18 percent, it should be noted clearly on the guest check at the time it is presented at the table.

In some parts of the country, however, this would be perceived as being somewhat "pushy" on the part of the innkeeper. Generally, a well-composed, discreetly placed tipping policy card in the guest room will be more positively greeted by your guest. Many innkeepers prefer to leave tipping decisions such as how much and to whom completely up to the guest's discretion.

A small policy card might read:

"Welcome. We are honored to have you as our guest. Many people have asked us how staff gratuities should be handled. We believe that service is a profession, and that tips for value-added services should be presented completely at the guest's discretion. NO AUTOMATIC SER-VICE FEES, CHARGES OR TIPS are added to any of the services here at THE RAINTREE INN. Any tips you choose to offer your maid and/or your dining room server will be graciously received and warmly appreciated."

Charlie and Deedy Marble in the dining room of the Governor's Inn, Ludlow, Vermont.

JÜRGEN SCHULTZ

Chapter Fifteen

CASH FLOW MANAGEMENT

The Off-Season

The Gift Shop

THE OFF-SEASON

Regardless of how successful you were in your "other" life, or how successful you are at developing an exciting and successful grand opening for your country inn, you might as well prepare yourself for the fact there will be some lean cash times ahead. All businesses have them, and innkeeping is no exception. There are a few tips, however, for making certain you are ready for the "low season" when it strikes your inn.

First, if you have done your planning well, the off-season should come as no surprise to you. Very few inns have a straightline occupancy percentage year round, and careful preopening research into your own market trends will reveal the natural ups and downs in the area. Once you are operating, keep concise and accurate records, month in and month out. It is an innkeeping fact of life that you cannot know where you are headed unless you have a clear idea of where you have been.

With your own projections in hand you can take steps to smooth out the peaks and valleys in the inn's cash flow. If you have substantial annual or semi-annual payments for such things as property tax or insurance, then they shouldn't surprise you each time they come due. Set aside a reserve account for each periodically recurring expense item and discipline yourself to make regular monthly or semi-monthly installments into that account. Pay attention to those purveyors who offer solid cash discounts for early payment, and schedule your bill paying accordingly.

Prudent attention to the use of revolving credit and charge accounts can save you many hundreds of dollars each year. One perfectly legal and equitable way to use the "float" in your own favor is to look at each charge card you carry and note the closing date on each account. Write those on a 3-by-5-inch card and set it aside in a convenient place for future reference. When you need to make a substantial credit card purchase, and you have some latitude about when the purchase is actually made, always try to make the purchase immediately following the closing date for billing on that particular credit card. Many cards do not begin charging interest until the month following the next posting and billing. If you pay your card off by its due date, approximately sixty days after your purchase, you have effectively had the use of the credit card company's funds interest-free for two months.

All fresh-faced new innkeepers find it difficult even to consider the idea of shutting down the operation for a regularly planned vacation each year. That's understandable. But you may very well discover that it is simply not cost-effective to operate the business on a "full steam ahead" basis when there is no business to be had. The fact is that Vermont has its "mud season" and every area of the country has a similar slow period — some slower and some longer than others. And whether you care to admit it now or not, the time away from innkeeping on a regularly scheduled basis each year will go a long way toward preserving your sanity and avoiding the possibility of burnout.

Put a little creative energy into exploring how many different goods and services that are regularly required by the inn can be negotiated on a barter rather than a cash basis. Often, the local florist, handyman, plumber, and even attorney will consider taking some or all of their compensation in guest room and dining room gift certificates. Although the widely accepted practice of bartering is the accountant's nightmare, it is still a viable and in some areas quite heavily used method of stretching each operating cash dollar.

THE GIFT SHOP

The primary additional source of cash within the inn, aside from guest room sales, dining room sales, and the sale of gift certificates, will come from your operation of the inn's own gift shop. The term gift shop has been interpreted throughout the industry to mean everything from a separate room adjacent to the common area of the inn to a nicely appointed corner of the foyer with a baker's rack display of inn mementos. Whichever approach you take, it is important that your gift shop area be well defined, well stocked, and offer an enticing cross-section of low to moderately priced gift items from the inn and the area.

A word of caution is in order here, and it pertains to ordering. A modestly successful gift shop operation that contributes regularly to the inn's cash flow can be devastated by one or two poorly timed or ill-advised buying decisions. Do not make the mistake of buying items that devour your cash up front, take up scarce space for inventory, and take forever to liquidate — just because they can accommodate your logo. You will be out of business long before you acquire a complete collection of everything that can be screen-printed, embroidered, or monogrammed for your inn.

Like all the other operating aspects of your inn, your gift shop requires a considerable amount of preparation and planning if it is going to succeed. A proper balance of locally produced arts and crafts, indus-try-specific inn materials such as inn videos, cookbooks, and guide-books, and assorted memorabilia thematically anchored to your inn will contribute handsomely to your overall cash flow.

Behind the Curtains . . .

The Governor's Inn, Ludlow, Vermont • Charlie and Deedy Marble.

The Governor's Inn offers eight guest rooms tastefully fur-nished with family antiques. Deedy and Charlie like sharing their inn and both of them work hard to evoke a more thoughtful, gentler, and softer era. The house was originally constructed by a former Vermont governor, William Wallace Stickney, who built the home as a wedding present for his wife, Elizabeth Lincoln. The Governor's Inn is located on Main Street in this village of 2,500 people, at the foot of a popular ski resort, Okemo Mountain. The Marbles bought the inn in 1982 and just celebrated their tenth anniversary of operation.

"I guess the biggest lesson we've learned over the years is flexibility. In order to survive when we began our business in 1982, we disciplined ourselves to adhere to very rigid rules of business and self-imposed policies from which we rarely deviated. With our experience and changing consumer tastes and behavior in the '90s we've evolved into a much more 'go with the flow' way of life.

"If we hadn't had the self-discipline to build in some time away from the business we might never have gotten around to nurtur-ing and developing additional inn management. We had to intro-duce the assistant innkeepers to the responsibilities of running the entire facility in small and measured doses. In the beginning, we separated the inn and the food and beverage area responsibili-ties and let our management trainees fully master both areas separately prior to assigning them overall responsibility for the entire property. It's not easy to entrust the facility to someone else, but in our experience it has been a healthy and intelligent business decision which we probably should have made five or six years earlier.

"I really love challenging myself in our kitchen and our suc-cesses in the fine dining side of our operation have played a major role in our success. I feel confident our dining facilities made it possible for us to earn the Mobil 4 Star rating, and to maintain a consistently strong reputation for creative, healthful, and interesting cuisine. Our guest rooms are lovely, but small. Without our dining facilities, we would be a completely different kind of business — and I don't think it would be nearly as much fun.

"When guests leave our inn we'd like them to depart with a feeling that they've been swept back in time. We hope they'll feel pampered by the warm and generous hospitality of our inn, and they will have completely forgotten the cares of their work week. We hope they leave us appreciative of their time in a beautiful place surrounded by special things and caring people. On a less esoteric level, we also hope our guests leave with a strong feeling of value for the discretionary money they've spent with us. We try not to forget that, particularly in tougher economic times, our guests have chosen to spend their time and money at our inn — and we are honored by their choice.

"Our 'typical' day is a great example of our division of labor. My husband is a morning person and I'm a night person so it works out great for us. Our day really begins the night before when the staff prepares the dining room by setting the tables for the appropriate number of guests. Since we already know how many we are going to serve, we are able to set the dining room accordingly. This avoids the big hotel dining room syndrome of having some tables set with no diners in sight. Since the tables are already set, we're off to a head start in the morning. We often serve a hot cereal, which we cook on a very low heat all night in our slow cooker. By cooking for a long period at a low heat the cereal releases all the gluten from the grain and dramatically improves the finished taste of the dish.

"My husband wakes up around 6:00 A.M. and begins preparing for the guests' breakfast. By 7:45 our staff arrives and changes into the period costumes they wear here at the inn. When the guests begin coming downstairs for the 8:00 A.M. seating, they are greeted by a table already set with the antique serving bell they ring when they are ready for us to begin serving coffee, tea, or hot chocolate. Since breakfast is generally the last experience our guest has here at the inn, we always try to make sure it is beautiful, flavorful, and bountiful, so their last impression is a lasting impression.

"While breakfast progresses in the dining room, I am still upstairs beginning my day at a considerably slower pace. Around 9:30 I come down to an absolutely pristine kitchen. (No, that's not something I taught him — I attribute it to good breeding!) By the time I come down, the guests are generally preparing to leave for their day's activities in the area or checking out, so we have an opportunity to schmooze before they leave.

"I begin cooking for our evening meal service, which we also serve to the public, at around 10:30 in the morning. At midday I break away from the prep process long enough to prepare lunch for our staff. We place a great deal of importance on providing both a hot breakfast and a hot lunch for whoever is on duty at the time. We actually sit down and eat together whenever we possibly can. Our staff dining policy is an important perk, and one which our employees have grown to really appreciate. They are served off the clock but their meals are served at no charge to them."

"By 2:00 in the afternoon I generally have our dinner pretty much in the final stages and we are able to focus on the mail. Like a lot of innkeepers, we really love to get our mail. It's usually a heavy load for our mailman so I'm sure he's as glad to leave it as we are to get it! Our mail is our primary means of keeping up with the rest of the folks in our industry through newsletters, advertising, and correspondence. Generally my husband and I try to grab a few minutes of midafternoon rest before we deal with the final preparation of dinner. It's during this hour or so that we try to read the industry-related mail and discuss whatever business matters we feel are necessary.

"While we're upstairs, our assistant innkeeper handles greeting our incoming guests and serves our afternoon tea. This first contact with the guest is critically important because it sets the pace and the level of expectation for the rest of the guest's stay. We spend a considerable amount of time training the employee and emphasizing the importance of this first contact, before we entrust the check-in procedure to him or her. If for some reason our assistant innkeeper is unavailable, then my husband or I will greet the arriving guests.

"I come back downstairs at approximately 5:00 P.M. and relieve our assistant innkeeper. After we have tidied up after our tea service, I return to the kitchen and complete the final preparation of dinner. I believe strongly that any inn operation that takes the dinner portion of their day seriously should have a quiet time the hour before dinner is served. Invariably, if the kitchen is a madhouse of frenzied last-minute detail within sixty minutes of serving the guest, it's too late! I realize this takes some getting used to, but believe me once you've developed the culinary discipline to prepare for your dinner appropriately, you'll never fall back into the last minute rush mayhem.

"At about 5 minutes before 7:00 I go into the parlor, greet each guest by name, and accompany them to their table in the dining room. Once again, in addition to making them feel comfortable, I am carefully observing their non-verbal behavior to make certain all is well with them and their visit. If the innkeeper learns that a guest has had a bad experience only as the guest is leaving, then the innkeeper has not been paying attention. One of the major competitive advantages of operating an inn with only eight or nine guest rooms is that we have the opportunity to focus on each guest, and to reinforce them subtly throughout their stay.

"As a kind of prelude to dinner, once we've seated everyone, I address them as a group and introduce them to each of the service staff who join me in the dining room. We extend a welcome to the assembled diners and describe the evening's meal and the wine we've recommended to accompany the selections. This might sound a little 'showy' for some innkeepers, but we take a lot of pride in the show business appeal of our operation. All of our service staff are in period costumes and we have fun capturing the complete essence of the dining experience.

"Dinner at our inn takes approximately two hours. When dinner is complete the guests adjourn to the parlor for an after-dinner brandy or liqueur prior to retiring for the evening. My husband generally goes to bed an hour or two before I do so he can be fresh as a daisy for breakfast the next morning.

"We go out of our way to make our guest feel special. Right from the start when the guest checks in we offer a little gift of welcome. When we turn down the guest's bed, we leave a flower and a foil-wrapped chocolate with the imprint of our inn in a small woven basket. Then at check-out we have still another parting gift. Admittedly, these are small gestures, but we're aware that not all inns go to those extra ends to make their guests feel special, so it makes every little thing we do that much more important, and that much more memorable."

TAMARA BROWN

The parlor of the Gastonian in Savannah, Georgia, is a feast for the senses.

Chapter Sixteen

TOUCH THE SENSES FOR SUCCESS

Touch

Sight

Smell and Sound

Taste

S uccessful country innkeepers never stop searching for new and better ways to "touch" the lives of their guests. Whether it is a wonderfully aromatic and regularly freshened potpourri, or a bi-monthly newsletter that keeps the inn's regular guests up to date, the touching seems never to end.

As an innkeeper you will invariably find yourself borrowing ideas from other hosts and hostesses you've encountered throughout your life. Here is a potpourri of useful ideas to start your collection.

TOUCH

The Clifton Inn in Charlottesville, Virginia, begins appealing to your senses literally from the moment you touch the front doorknob. Care-fully laced and hand-tied to the front door, in such a way that you cannot open the door without squeezing the fragrant sprigs, is a small bunch of fresh rosemary. When you open the door the aroma of fresh-cut rosemary is gently imparted to your fingers.

Since much of the touching that goes on in the inn will involve the guest sitting on, or in, the inn's furniture, it's a good idea to furnish your facility for comfort and function as well as form. Many country inns take pride in furnishing their premises with historically accurate an-tiques that may look wonderful but actually feel terrible. Before acquir-ing a piece of furniture for your inn, consider whether you plan for it to be actually used by your guests. If it will be used, then take the time to sit in the chair or lie on the mattress to find out how this part of your guest's inn experience will actually feel.

The sense of touch conveyed by your inn extends to the overall environment as well. Not everyone is comfortable in a room that is kept at a constant temperature of 75 degrees. Be sensitive to the body language of your guests, and adjust your heating, cooling, and ventila-tion accordingly.

SIGHT

When a guest arrives at your country inn, his or her first impression will not be of the inn, but of the grass, trees, bushes, flowers, and landscaping that surround it. In addition, if the road, driveway, or lane that leads to your front door is poorly maintained, filled with potholes, tree limbs, trash, and badly in need of some fundamental repair, you may have lost the good first impression battle before it is ever begun.

What else does the guest scrutinize before he or she ever arrives at your front door? The inn's sign. Nothing is a clearer indication of a substandard lodging facility than a sign with cracked, chipped, or peeling paint or burned-out/faulty lighting. A professionally painted and properly maintained sign goes a long way toward making a positive first impression.

An important part of the regularly scheduled maintenance and upkeep of your inn involves a careful exterior inspection, both in the daytime and in the evening. Stand outside your inn and scrutinize it carefully for chipping paint, torn screens, dead plants, etc. When you have finished that inspection, do it once again in the evening with all the lights on. Pay particularly close attention to burned-out or missing light bulbs . . . even in the hard to reach places!

Once your guest parks his or her car and begins to approach the front door, what's the first thing that is going to be noticed? Often it will be the porch or entryway furniture and accessories you have selected for the inn. The area outside the front door must be inviting. This means a freshly swept walkway or front porch, and seasonal furniture that seems to say, "Welcome . . . come and enjoy our inn."

"Throughout our inn we try to leave the impression of generous and bountiful hospitality, and we try to touch all the senses in the process. When you come through our front door and into our small alcove, you'll immediately notice the seasonal potpourri scent which we keep constantly refreshed and rescented. Our fruit baskets and tea service are always above and beyond in quantity and freshness. Upstairs in the hall off the guest rooms, we have a large basket which we call a 'silent butler.' We've placed small sample sizes of everything from shoe shine kits to shaving cream, toothbrushes, combs, dental floss, mouthwash, wet naps, and virtually every imaginable and occasionally forgotten little necessity. In recent years, we've even begun adding condoms to the basket as our gesture of social consciousness and concern for the well-being of our guests."

When the guest arrives at the front door, do not assume he or she will automatically know what to do. If you plan to answer the doorbell personally each time it rings, or to have it answered promptly by someone on your staff, then a discreetly placed sign inviting the guest to "Please ring the doorbell for the Innkeeper" will end any confusion. If you prefer to leave the door unlocked and to have the guest enter without using the bell or door knocker, then that too should be indicated discreetly at the entrance. The instruction signage need not be expensively engraved antique brass, but it should be tasteful and indicate some attention to detail.

In the hospitality business, when the topic turns to first impressions, it invariably revolves around the guest's initial contact with the host or hostess. The longer the guest has to wait to be greeted, the more unsure and uncomfortable he or she will feel. In only a few seconds, the mood of the guest can be changed from curiousity to uncertainty, and the rest of the experience at the facility may be viewed the same way.

SMELL AND SOUND

Behaviorists are only just beginning to understand what these two powerful senses have to do with mood, impressions, and perceptions. Like every other part of managing the way your inn is perceived, both sound and smell will require careful and regular attention on the part of the innkeeper. In recent years, a variety of scented candles, essence potpourris, stovetop potpourris, carpet powders, plugins, stickups, and sprays have been introduced to the marketplace. Once these products were used strictly to cover up distasteful cooking, smoking, or bathroom odors. As the fragrance industry has grown, however, so too has the selection of aromas and delivery systems available to the consumer.

As an innkeeper, you will want to try a variety of aromas and delivery systems, until you find the right combination for your facility. Often that might mean the combination which you and your staff find most pleasant day in and day out. It is difficult to duplicate with commercial scents the rich homey smell of a fresh apple pie baking in the oven, but that is the goal. Real estate agents have long known the effects of fresh-baked bread or pies on the perception of the person looking at a home for the first time. The same basic idea applies to welcoming a guest to your inn for the first time.

Whatever combination of scents you select, choose a delivery system that does not need hourly attention. As you experiment with the various methods of manipulating the aroma of your inn, don't overlook the natural scents you have at your fingertips. Freshly cut flowers, hot spiced tea, a bowl of apples, and a crackling fire of hickory or cedar split wood logs all impart an unmistakable natural aroma of home and hospitality.

The absence or presence of background music is one of those issues about which there is no middle ground. Successful country innkeepers either love the idea of a lilting Vivaldi string quartet playing in the background or they consider it an unwelcome intrusion on the serenity and solitude of the inn. With recent hardware developments now making it possible to play a series of selected compact disks in succession without having to bother with the equipment, the concept of pleasant background music makes more and more sense.

A high-quality compact disc system with volume controls in each common area room is not a terribly costly proposition. You might even wish to offer your guests the opportunity to select their favorite discs from your collection. The key point here is to make certain the only discs allowed even near the system are the ones you have selected to contribute to the peaceful atmosphere of the inn. Invariably, if you permit the kitchen or housekeeping staff to bring in their own discs and to play them when they are alone in the inn, you will end up hearing that very same music one afternoon during your carefully planned high tea presentation.

TASTE

The rule here, for the serious student of the food and beverage side of innkeeping, is that you are much better off doing a small number of food and beverage items very well than attempting to offer a large number of items in a so-so manner. It may be very tempting at first to "chase the requests" of your guests, but you will be glad if you resist the temptation to please everyone.

Food is first of all a matter of common sense. By thoroughly familiarizing youself with what is available in your area, at its freshest, and when, you begin to construct an outline for the types of dishes that will in all likelihood work best for your inn. In Weathersfield, Vermont, for example, a little-known but superb by-product of the annual apple cider-pressing is pure apple cider jelly, which is processed and jarred in very limited quantities by a small local cider house. This jelly is so rare and so special that the Inn at Weathersfield offers it for sale every year to its guests as a local signature item until the annual supply is exhausted.

That same inn also has a chef whose sideline is raising wild game for the table. Not surprisingly, the pheasant and other wild game served at Weathersfield have no peer in midtown Manhattan's best restaurants.

Beginning with fresh, locally available ingredients and a penchant for cooking, you have the basic ingredients of a country inn kitchen that can do anything — and go anywhere. One wonderfully creative country innkeeper named Crescent Dragonwagon carried her renowned Dairy Hollow House Inn all the way to the hallowed halls of Congress — as one of the featured chefs during President Bill Clinton's inaugural festivities.

Whether it is your favorite make-ahead breakfast casserole or your grandmother's "to-die" pineapple muffins, learn to prepare them consistently and well, before expanding your line of signature dishes to new horizons. Appealing to the taste of your guests need not be limited to breakfast, tea, and dinner. An abundant self-service fresh fruit basket, or a constantly replenished cookie jar with fresh baked cookies, or a simple "sweet" on the guest's pillow in the evening, are all equally important opportunities to appeal to the good taste of your guest. You will discover many others, and some may even become a historic custom at your inn like the tradition of serving cookies and hot chocolate on the front porch at Marshlands Inn, in Sackville, New Brunswick.

Behind the Curtains . . .

The Gastonian, Savannah, Georgia • Hugh and Roberta Lineberger.

The Gastonian began operation in 1985. Hugh and Roberta live in the inn and are best described as prototypically successful hands-on managers. A basket of fresh fruit and a split of wine always welcome the arriving guest at the Gastonian. A turndown service in the evening is accented with a touch of truly Southern hospitality, a delicious peach cordial, and Savannah pralines are always left on the pillow.

"In the mornings, a full, hot, sit-down table-service Southern-style breakfast is served in one or two seatings. My wife and I do all the cooking, with some occasional weekend help from one of the local college students who help out during our busy spring season. We take a lot of pride in not serving our guests the same breakfast twice during any given stay. We rotate thirteen or fourteen original recipes, and we're proud of the fact that several have turned up in such famous cookbooks as Better Homes and Gardens.

"In the seven years we've been open, we have never had one single guest who caused us to wish under our breath that they'd never return. It just has not happened. The people who visit our inn don't come here for a place to sleep. That's included, of course, but it is not the primary reason for them to choose our inn. The main reason they visit us is, that like the entire country, they are smitten by nostalgia, and they appreciate what we've done here to regenerate these nineteenth-century mansions.

"We are involved in this community in a very big way. My wife serves on the board of directors for her church, is the vice president of the local Republican Women's Club, and is on the board of directors of the Ladies Auxiliary for the Savannah Symphony Orchestra. I am on the Board of Governors of the local Chamber of Commerce, I sit on the board and serve as the director of marketing for our Savannah Convention and Visitors' Bureau, and I am on the boards of the Historic Savannah Foundation and the United Way. We take our local involvement very seriously, but we recognize that it is not an important bottom-line contributor to our business. We take an interest in our community and the history of the area just because we like to do it.

"Only a small fraction of our business actually comes from the local community. Twenty-five percent of our visiting guests come from Atlanta, with Orlando, Jacksonville, and Charleston following in that order. The balance of our business is spread all over the map. We do a considerable business with people who travel seasonally between the snowbound North and Florida. And with the dollar devaluation against foreign currencies in recent months, we've seen a sizeable increase in our international traffic.

"We generally get up at 5:30 and begin preparing breakfast for our guests. When we're full, which is most of the time, we have twenty-six people for breakfast. We generally set up two seatings at 8:00 and 10:00 A.M. Our breakfasts always include juice, fresh seasonal fruit, one hot entree, and some kind of sweet course.

"When our guests leave we make certain two things have happened. First, we make sure they have enjoyed themselves at our inn. It doesn't take a lot of insight to detect when something has not gone according to Hoyle. Since the lifeblood of our business is referral, we cannot afford to have someone leave us with a less than absolutely positive memory of their stay. Second, we consider it our job to sell Savannah to our guests. If we've done that job well, we've enhanced their perception of our inn in the process."

Conclusion

Let's face it. A lot of what any useful "how to" book must do is tell you what not to do. That is certainly as it should be, whether you are planning to open and operate a country inn, a fast-food franchise, or any other kind of business.

In the final analysis, the same pitfalls that all start-up businesses face are present in innkeeping. Poor preparation, lack of sufficient capital, and a bad location are all seeds for failure in innkeeping. If you have read this book carefully, you have already taken an initial step toward eliminating one of these pitfalls and preparing yourself for what lies ahead.

It is now time to toss this book into an overnight bag and begin researching the industry. Start your collection of experiences next weekend, by visiting a country inn. Begin keeping a diary or log of all your inn experiences, highlighting the most memorable parts of your stay along the way. Whether it's the pewter napkin rings, the unforgettable aroma of magnolia blossoms as you relax with your morning coffee on the front porch, the hand-written good-night note left on your pillow, the strains of Vivaldi filling a firefly-jeweled summer night, or that slightly decadent breakfast of a piping-hot baked apple topped with homemade ice cream, your treasury of country inn experiences will become a valuable foundation for your future life as an innkeeper.

You are on your way to becoming a member of a consortium of the most interesting people in the world . . . the keepers of inns. I look forward to crossing paths with you!

APPENDIX A

Associations

NATIONAL ASSOCIATIONS

The Independent Innkeeper's Association (IIA). Founded in 1972, IIA is an association of independent innkeepers who are dedicated to providing the guest with a unique hospitality experience by "being the best at what we do...individually and collectively." For membership qualifications, inspection criteria, and information on the Innkeepers' Register, write IIA, Box 150, Marshall, MI 49068, or call 800-344-5244.

Professional Association Of Innkeepers International (PAII) (pronounced PIE, as in Mom's Apple). PAII is the professional trade association for the country inn industry and a very good starting point for aspiring and current innkeepers. For membership information, contact PAII, P.O. Box 90710, Santa Barbara, CA 93190, or call 805-965-0707.

The American Bed & Breakfast Association (AB&BA), established in 1981, serves as the central clearinghouse for bed and breakfast, travel, and trade information in North America. The AB&BA offers a broad array of activities and programs. For a free sample membership packet, contact the AB&BA, 1407 Huguenot Road, Midlothian, VA 23113, or call 804-379-ABBA.

STATE AND REGIONAL ASSOCIATIONS

Note: Many of these associations are run by innkeepers. It is best to contact an association first by mail to learn how they operate and how they might best serve your needs. Remember, innkeepers, particularly those who volunteer to head their area professional associations, have extremely busy early mornings and mid-afternoons. If you plan to call, try them toward the middle of the day, and ask first if it might be convenient for them to spend a few minutes with you on the telephone.

We've worked hard to ensure the accuracy of all addresses and telephone numbers. If our roster is not current due to recent changes in an association, please let us know, and we'll make the appropriate changes in our future editions.

Alaska
Alaska Bed & Breakfast Association, 526 Seward Street, Juneau, AK 99801. 907-586-2959

Arizona
Arizona Association of B&B Inns, 3661 North Campbell Avenue, Box 237, Tucson, AZ 85719. 602-622-7167
Sedona B&B Innkeepers Guild, Box 552, Sedona, AZ 86336. 602-282-2833

Arkansas
Association of B&Bs of Eureka Springs, 82 Armstrong St., Eureka Springs, AR 72632
Bed & Breakfast Association of Arkansas, 303 Quapaw Avenue, Hot Springs, AR 71901. 501-623-3258

California
Association of B&B Innkeepers, San Francisco, 737 Buena Vista Way, San Francisco, CA 94117. 415-861-3008
Auburn Area B&B Inns, 601 Lincoln Way, Auburn, CA 95603. 916-885-5616
B&Bs of Amador County, 215 Court Street, Jackson, CA 95642. 209-223-0416
Mendocino Coast Innkeeper's Association, Box 1141, Mendocino, CA 95460. 707-877-3321

El Dorado County Innkeepers Association, Box 106, Placerville, CA 95667. 916-626-5840

B&B Innkeepers Guild of Santa Barbara, Box 90734, Santa Barbara, CA 93120

Inns of Point Reyes, Box 145, Point Reyes, CA 94965. 415-663-1420

B&B Innkeepers of Northern California, Box 715, Chico, CA 95927. 800-284-INNS

B&B Innkeepers of Santa Cruz, Box 464, Santa Cruz, CA 95061. 408-425-8212

B&B Inns of Humboldt County, Box 40, Ferndale, CA 95536. 707-786-4000

Gold Country Inns of Tuolumne County, Box 462, Sonora, CA 95370. 209-553-1845

Historic Country Inns of the Mother Lode, Box 502, Coloma, CA 95613. 916-622-6919

Monterey Peninsula B&B Association, 500 Martin Street, Monterey, CA 93940. 408-375-5284

Sacramento Innkeepers Association, 2120 G Street, Sacramento, CA 95816. 916-441-5007

Wine Country Inns of Sonoma County, Box 51, Geyserville, CA 95441. 707-533-INNS

Yosemite B&Bs of Mariposa Country, Box 1100, Mariposa, CA 95338

Colorado

B&B Innkeepers of Colorado, 1102 West Pikes Peak Avenue, Colorado Springs, CO 80904. 719-471-3980

Association of Historic Hotels of the Rocky Mountains, 3391 South Race Street, Englewood, CO 80110

Colorado Inn Association, Box 10472, Colorado Springs, CO 80932. 800-866-0621

Western Slope B&B Association, Box 433, Wheatbridge, CO 80033. 303-856-6066

Connecticut

B&B Inns of Connecticut, 96 Tucker Hill Road, Middlebury, CT 06762. 203-758-8334

Delaware
Delaware Association of B&Bs & Biking Inn To Inn, Route 1, Box 283, Laurel, DE 19956. 302-875-7015

Georgia
Georgia B&B Council, 326 Greene Street, Augusta, GA 30901. 800-241-2407
Savannah Inn Association, 29 Abercorn Street, Savannah, GA 31401

Hawaii
B&B Homestay Proprietors Association of Hawaii, 1277 Mokulu Drive, Kailua, HI 96734. 808-261-1059

Idaho
Idaho B&B Innkeepers Association, P.O. Box 2503, Coeur d'Alene, ID 83814. 208-689-3630
B&B Association of Inland Northwest, Box 2503, Coeur d'Alene, ID 83814. 406-847-5597

Indiana
Indiana B&B Association, 350 Indian Boundary Road, Chesterton, IN 46304. 219-926-5781

Iowa
Dubuque Area B&Bs, 1072 West Third Street, Dubuque, IO 52001
Iowa B&B Innkeepers Association, 629 First Avenue East, Newton, IO 50208. 515-792-6833

Kansas
Kansas B&B Association, 1675 West Patterson Avenue, Ulysses, KS 67880

Kentucky
B&B of Kentucky, Route 3-B, Box 20, Springfield, KY 40069. 606-336-3075

Maine
Inns of the Island, Box 353, Bar Harbor, ME 04609. 207-288-9439
Maine Innkeeepers Association, 142 Free Street, Portland, ME 04101. 207-773-7670

Maine Farm Vacation & B&B Association, Box 4, Bristol Mills, ME
    04539

Maryland
Annapolis Association of Licensed B&B Owners, Box 744,
    Annapolis, MD 21404. 301-263-6418
Maryland Regional Association, 8 Martin Street, Annapolis, MD
    21401
B&B Inns of the Eastern Shore, 1500 Hambrooks Blvd., Cambridge,
    MD 21613. 301-228-0575
Chesapeake Inns, Box 609, Chestertown, MD 21620. 301-778-INNS
Inns of the Blue Ridge, 19 East Church Street, Frederick, MD 21701.
    301-633-8703
Maryland B&B Association, Box 23324, Baltimore, MD 21203.
    301-225-0001

Massachusetts
Association of Massachusetts B&Bs, Box 341, West Hyannisport, MA
    02672. 508-775-2772
Hampshire Hills B&B Association, Box 553, Worthington, MA
    01098. 413-296-4363
In The Country B&B Association, Box 23, Buckland, MA 01338.
    413-625-2975
Nantucket Lodging Association, 7 East Sea Street, Nantucket, MA
    02554. 508-228-3577

Michigan
B&B Grand Traverse, 622 Washington Street, Traverse City, MI
    49684
B&Bs of Saugatuck, Box 1123, Saugatuck, MI 49453. 616-857-4535
Heartland Triangle, Box 546, Brooklyn, MI 49230
Lake to Lake B&B Association, Route 2 Box 183, Cedar, MI 49621.
    616-288-7014

Minnesota
Minnesota B&B Association, 11600 Indian Beach Road, Spicer, MN
    56288. 612-796-5870
North Shore B&B Association, Box 181, Grand Marais, MN 55604.
    800-622-4014

Minnesota Historic B&B Association, 4th and Pine Street, Hastings, MN 55033. 612-437-3297
Minnesota B&B Guild, 306 West Olive, Stillwater, MN 55082. 612-430-2955

Missouri
Bed & Breakfast Inns of Missouri, Garth Woodside Mansion, R.R. 1, Hannibal, MO 63401. 314-221-2789

Nebraska
Nebraska Association of B&Bs, Box 22333, Lincoln, NE 68542. 402-423-3480

Nevada
Northern Nevada B&B Guild, 1201 Winters Creek Ranch, U.S. 395, Carson City, Nevada 89701. 792-849-1020

New Hampshire
Hearths & Hillsides B&B Association, Box 2025, North Conway, NH 03860. 800-562-1300
New England Innkeeper's Association, Box 1089, North Hampton, NH 03862. 603-964-6689
Monadnock Region Inns & B&Bs, Box 236, Jaffrey, NH 03452

New Jersey
Inns Along the Coast, 22 Lakeside Avenue, Avon-by-the-Sea, NJ 07717. 201-776-8727
Ocean City Innkeepers Association, 1020 Central Avenue, Ocean City, NJ 98226

New Mexico
New Mexico B&B Association, Box 2925, Santa Fe, NM 87504
Taos B&B Association, Box 2772, Taos, NM 87571. 505-758-4747

New York
B&B Association of Saratoga, Lake George, and Gore Mountain, Box 99, Lake Lucerne, NY 12846. 518-696-9912
Finger Lakes B&B Association, Box 862, Canandaigua, NY 14424. 607-547-6290

B&B Leatherstocking, Central New York, R.D. 1, Box 80, Mohawk, NY 13407. 315-866-1306

North Carolina
North Carolina B&B Association, 509 Pollock Street, New Bern, NC 28560. 919-636-5553

Ohio
B&B in the Hills of Southern Ohio, P.O. Box 350, Logan, OH 43138. 614-385-5713
Association of Ohio B&B Homes and Inns, 29683 Walhonding Avenue, Danville, OH 43014. 614-599-6107

Oregon
Ashland B&B Network, Box 1051, Ashland, OR 97520. 503-482-BEDS
Columbia River Gorge B&B Association, 4000 Westcliff Drive, Hood River, OR 97031 503-386-5566
Oregon B&B Guild, Box 3187, Ashland, OR 97520
Unique Northwest Inns, Box 429, Donald, OR 97207. 503-386-5566
Portland Innkeepers, Box 69292, Portland, OR 97202

Pennsylvania
B&B Association of the Delaware River Valley, Box 215, New Hope, PA 18938. 215-794-5254
B&B Division, Pennsylvania Travel Council, 111 W. Bridge Street, New Hope, PA 18938. 215-862-2570
North Central Pennsylvania Association, 439 Market Street, Lewisburg, PA 17837. 717-464-5881
Inns of the Gettysburg Area, Box 3273, Gettysburg, PA 17235, 800-247-2216
Pennsylvania Travel Council, 902 North Second Street, Harrisburg, PA 17102. 717-232-8880
Lancaster County B&B Inns Association, 2835 Willow Street Pike, Willow Street, PA 17584. 717-464-5881

Rhode Island
Newport Historic Inns, Box 981, Newport, RI 02840. 401-846-5444
Newport County B&B Association, 22 Channing Street, Newport, RI 02840.

Tennessee
East Tennessee B&B Inns & Lodges Association, 315 Main Street,
   Greeneville, TN 37743. 615-638-2917
Tennessee B&B Innkeepers Association, 3313 South Circle,
   Knoxville, TN 37920. 615-579-4508

Texas
East Texas B&B Association, 1160 North Highway 19, Canton, TX
   75103. 214-567-2899
Historic Hotel Association, 501 West Main St., Fredericksburg, TX
   78624. 512-997-3980
B&B Society of Texas, 7114 Eicher, Houston, TX 77036.
   713-771-3939
B&B of Wimberley, Box 259, Wimberley, TX 78676, 512-847-9666

Utah
B&B Inns of Utah, Inc., Box 2639, Park City, UT 84060.
   801-645-8068

Vermont
Historic Inns of Norman Rockwell's Vermont, Box 203, Arlington,
   VT 05250. 802-375-2269

Virginia
B&B Association of Virginia, Route 1, Box 533, Wirtz, VA 24184.
   703-721-3951
Historic Inns of Charlottesville, Box 5737, Charlottesville, VA
   22905. 804-979-7264
Inns of the Northern Neck, Box 425, Irvington, VA 22480.
   804-438-6053
Rappahannock B&B Guild, Route 1, Box 2080, Flint Hill, VA 22627.
   703-675-3693
Shenandoah Valley Historic B&Bs, Route 2, Box 155, Mount
   Crawford, VA 22841
Virginia Inns of the Shenandoah Valley, Box 918, Hot Springs,
   VA 24445

Washington
Association of Special Places, Box 378, Issaquah, WA 98027.
   206-392-0451

B&B Association of San Juan Island, 4531-A Cattle Point Road, Friday Harbor, WA 98250. 206-378-3186

B&B of Bellingham & Whatcom County, 4421Lakeway Drive, Bellingham, WA 98226. 206-733-0055

B&B of Spokane Association, East 627 Twenty Fifth Street, Spokane, WA 99203. 509-624-3776

Fidalgo Island B&B Guild, 4911 MacBeth Drive, Anacortes, WA 98221. 206-293-4792

Island B&B Inns of Distinction, Route 1, Box 1940, Lopez Island, WA 98261. 206-468-2253

Leavenworth Area B&B Association, Box 285, Leavenworth, WA 98826. 509-548-7171

Olympic Peninsula B&B Association, 731 Pierce, Port Townsend, WA 98368. 206-385-4168

Seattle B&B Association, Box 95853, Seattle, WA 98145. 206-547-1020

Washington B&B Guild, 2442 NW Market Street, Suite 355, Seattle, WA 98107

Whidbey Island B&B Association, Box 259, Langley WA 98260. 206-678-3115

Wisconsin

B&B Association of Wisconsin, 458 Glenway Street, Madison, WI. 53711

B&B Innkeepers Association of Wisconsin's Hidden Valleys, 220 East Franklin Street, Sparta, WI 54656. 608-269-3894

Wisconsin B&B Homes & Historic Inns, Route 1, Box 263, Sparta, WI 54656. 608-269-4522

APPENDIX B

NEWSLETTERS

The Discerning Traveler. This limited-circulation newsletter reviews one city or region in each issue. Published bi-monthly by The Discerning Traveler, 504 West Mermaid Lane, Philadelphia, PA 19118. 215-247-5578

Norm Strasma's Inn Marketing. Information for innkeepers about innkeepers, focusing on marketing. Published monthly except August and December by Norman and Janice Strasma, Box 1789, Kankakee, IL 60901. 815-939-3509

Innkeeping. The monthly newsletter for owners and operators of bed and breakfast and country inns is published by the Professional Association of Innkeepers International, Box 90710, Santa Barbara, CA 93190. 805-569-1853

INNroads. A new quarterly from Sandra Soule, talented author of the widely acclaimed book series *America's Wonderful Little Hotels & Inns*. Box 150, Riverside, CT 06878. 203-637-7642

Midwest Innkeepers Newsletter. Another new quarterly that combines innkeeping news from the eight states comprising the heartland of America. 105 E. Court Street, Box 1789, Kankakee, IL 60901. 815-939-3509 or FAX: 815-933-8320

Shoptalk. The bi-monthly newsletter of the American Bed & Breakfast Association, 10800 Midlothian Turnpike, Suite 254, Richmond, VA 23235. 804-379-2222 or FAX: 804-379-1469

Tidings. The bi-monthly member publication of the Independent Innkeepers' Association, Box 150, Marshall, Michigan 49068. 616-789-0393

Index

About the Author

C. Vincent Shortt is a highly re-garded expert in the field of hospi-tality industry marketing, an award-winning film and television producer, and creator of the hit Cable TV lifestyles series, "Great Country Inns." He is also Executive Producer of the "Inn Country USA" television series and the author of the forthcoming companion book based on the series, *The Innkeep-ers' Collection,* a treasury of recipes from the private files of America's most successful inns.